THE BEGINNING OF KNOWLEDGE

Hans-Georg Gadamer

THE
BEGINNING
OF
KNOWLEDGE

Translated by Rod Coltman

CONTINUUM
NEW YORK • LONDON

2002

The Continuum International Publishing Group Inc
370 Lexington Avenue, New York, NY 10017

The Continuum International Publishing Group Ltd
The Tower Building, 11 York Road, London SE1 7 NX

Original published as *Der Anfang des Wissens*
Copyright © 1999 by J.C.B. Mohr (Paul Siebeck), Tübingen,
except for the "Einleitung" and "Der Naturbegriff und die
Naturwissenschaft," which are copyright by Philipp Reclam jun.
GmbH & Co., Stuttgart

English translation copyright © 2001
by The Continuum International Publishing Group

Printed in the United States of America

Library of Congress Cataloging-in-Publication Data

Gadamer, Hans Georg, 1900–
    [Anfang des Wissens, English]
    The beginning of knowledge / Hans-Georg Gadamer;
    translated by Rod Coltman.
        p.   cm.
    Includes bibliographical references and index.
    ISBN 0–8264–1195–9
    1. Pre-Socratic philosophers.   I. Title.
B187.5.G33513   2001
182–dc21   2001042544

Contents

Translator's Preface

In his autobiographical sketch, *Philosophical Apprenticeships*,[1] Gadamer tell us that, even while studying with Heidegger in Marburg, Paul Friedländer was teaching him to read Plato as a literary writer and not just a philosophical one. And while his 'Heideggerization' was to profoundly determine the course of his own philosophical development, Gadamer's doctoral training under Paul Natorp had already placed him within a Platonic horizon from within which he would appropriate and interpret the phenomenological ontology of his new mentor. This, of course, is why (working against the Heideggerian idea of a monolithic 'history of metaphysics' in need of dismantling) Gadamer can situate such figures as Plato and Hegel at the center of his philosophical hermeneutics. I would also argue that this early philological training combined with his own literary sensibilities allow Gadamer to emerge as a deeply Platonic thinker—not in the traditional sense of a teleological metaphysician but in the literary sense, that of a writer who is keenly attuned to the structure and movement of language.

To illustrate what I mean, let us briefly examine Plato's role in his own dialogues—not just as the writer, not as a character per se or as a direct interlocutor, and certainly not in terms of the simplistic identification of Socrates with Plato that plagues traditional Platonistic readings and even many extremely sophisticated (pun intended) contemporary analyses of the dialogues. Plato, I would argue, is omnipresent in these philosophical dramas. He is indeed, as most Plato scholars would have it, Socrates and the Eleatic stranger, but he is also Glaucon and Adeimantus, Euthyphro and Meletus, and even Callicles and Thrasymachus.

1. Translated by Robert R. Sullivan, Cambridge: MIT Press, 1985. Originally published as *Philosophische Lehrjahre: Eine Rückschau*, Frankfurt a. M., Klostermann, 1977.

He is Gorgias and Protagoras and Parmenides himself. He is even the cicadas singing in the Plato trees, watching over Socrates' pastoral and erotic encounter with Phaedrus as well as Diotima, the wise woman of Mantinea who taught Socrates the art of love. All of these are literally Plato's voices in that he wrote their words, but they are also his voices in that the interlocutors' interactions with Socrates (or whoever is leading a given discussion), far from being superfluous, not only determine the direction of the conversation but the ideas presented by these other characters, even by Socrates' 'antagonists,' are frequently not simply undermined or destroyed but (to mix dialectics) *aufgehoben*, sublated, only to reemerge as a crucial facet of a later dialogical construct.[2]

I am trying to suggest here that Gadamer's profound understanding of the literary as well as the philosophical aspects of the Platonic dialogue manifests itself in all of his own writings. Gadamer will be the first to admit that he is not the literary genius that Plato was (whom Gadamer puts on a par with Goethe and Shakespeare), but we can perhaps think of him as something of a historical genius. That is, insofar as he *theorizes* about what he calls 'effective history' (*Wirkungsgeschichte*), he also *depicts* it (or perhaps 'enacts' it) in each and every one of his texts, and this is certainly as true of his elucidations of historical figures in shorter pieces such as the ones presented here as it is of his more elaborate explications of his own philosophical attitude such as we find in *Truth and Method*. Unlike Plato's virtuosic polyphony, however, Gadamer's voices are not those of contemporary figures placed into fictional contexts for philosophical and pedagogical effect, but those of historical figures situated in their own hermeneutical contexts for philosophical and pedagogical effect.

Gadamer's primary voices, his primary muses, his three-headed Socrates, if you will, are Heidegger, Hegel, and Plato. His Heideggerian voice is expressed or 'brought to language'[3] in his historical, phenomenological, and ontological interpretation of consciousness. His Hegelian voice is brought to language in his

---

2. The most obvious example being Polemarchus' idea, in the *Republic*, of doing good to one's friends and harm to one's enemies.

3. 'Zur Sprache gebracht,' as the German locution so eloquently puts it.

historical and speculative/dialectical understanding of the movement of *die Sache selbst* and the occurrence of the phenomenon of understanding as a non-teleological *Aufhebung* that
arises not in logical propositions but in live conversation. And
Gadamer's Platonic voice comes to language in both his dia-
logical/dialectical interpretation of history and the analogical
pedagogy of his historical presentations of philosophical figures.

And this, I think, is crucial for understanding Gadamer's
other voices—Kant, Herder, Schleiermacher, Dilthey, Augustine,
Aquinas, Aristotle, and, of course (for the purposes of the present volume), Heraclitus, Parmenides, Democritus, and the other
so-called Presocratics: Gadamer's pedagogy, like Plato's, is frequently analogical but never didactic. Just as Plato allows the dra-
matic setting and the personalities of the interlocutors to drive the
discourse of the dialogues, which must always take 'the longer
way' if it is to be effective,[4] Gadamer's project has always been
to allow the tortuous trajectory of what he calls 'the forgetfulness
of language' to show itself throughout the history of philosophical discourse. In other words, whether he is 'theorizing
about' philosophical hermeneutics, as in *Truth and Method*, or
'applying it,' as he does in the essays below—if such a distinction
makes any real hermeneutical sense—Gadamer is always and
everywhere concerned with the lack of sensitivity to language and
context that characterizes most traditional scholarship. But, of
course, what is forgotten is not gone, only covered over, hidden;
and in large part, the essays presented in this volume bring
Gadamer's immense philological acumen to bear on a question
with enormous philosophical and even scientific consequences—
specifically, the question of the extent to which the tradition
itself has largely forgotten (or at least missed) the fact that
linguistic as well as historical, cultural, political, and religious
contexts have determined and continue to determine our understanding of philosophical thought before Plato.

The pieces translated and presented here function as a sort of
companion volume to *The Beginning of Philosophy*,[5] at least

---

4. In fact, if we look closely, we can discern one of Plato's favorite
analogies operating in many of the dialogues—i.e., the idea that, just as
Odysseus learns only by following the tortuous path laid out for him by
Moira, the conversation must be allowed to sail wherever the wind takes it.
5. New York: Continuum International Publishing Group, 1998;

to the extent that here, too, Gadamer offers us a series of philo-
logically and philosophically grounded interpretations of Presocratic thought by penetrating the veneer of the doxographical
tradition from which we have inherited these testimonies and to
the extent that, together, these two little books represent the
only two extended publications on the Presocratics in Gadamer's
entire corpus to date. However, their own rather more straightforward doxographical history sets these essays apart from those
of the previous volume. The earlier texts were a series of previously unpublished lectures that were originally offered as
a lecture course in 1967, reworked and delivered publically
in Italian in 1988, and then transcribed and edited for publi-
cation in Italy in 1993 before being translated back into German
for republication in 1996. All of the present essays (except for
the Author's Preface) have appeared in print elsewhere, and all
but the last piece are included in Gadamer's 10-volume *Gesammelte Werke*.[6]

The philosophical focus of *The Beginning of Knowledge*[7]
is also slightly different from that of *The Beginning of Philosophy*. As the word 'knowledge' (*Wissen*) in the title suggests,
here Gadamer is not so much interested in the origins of philosophy per se but rather those of knowledge in general—or at
least its origins in the Western tradition. In *The Beginning of
Knowledge*, Gadamer reminds us that philosophy for the Greeks
was not just a question of metaphysics and epistemology, but it
also encompassed cosmology, physics, mathematics, medicine,
and the entire reach of theoretical curiosity and intellectual mastery—everything, that is, that we call 'science' and the Germans
call 'Wissenschaft.' Whereas *The Beginning of Philosophy* deals
with the inception of philosophical inquiry as such by focusing
primarily on the history of the reception and interpretation
of Parmenides' didactic poem, *The Beginning of Knowledge*
brings together nearly all of Gadamer's previously published

originally published in German as *Der Anfang der Philosophy*, Stuttgart:
Reclam, 1996.
   6. Tübingen: J. C. B. Mohr (Paul Siebeck), 1985–1991, hereafter
referred to as GW, followed by volume and page numbers. (A complete list
of textual citations appears at the end of this volume).
   7. Originally published in German as *Der Anfang des Wissens*,
Stuttgart: Reclam, 1999.

(but never before translated) essays on the Presocratics. Beginning with two hermeneutical and philological investigations of the Heraclitus fragments that are rather similar in scope to his previous analyses of Parmenides ("On the Heraclitus Tradition," from 1974, and "Heraclitus Studies," from 1990), he then moves on to one of his very earliest pieces, a discussion of the Greek atomists ("Ancient Atomic Theory," 1935) and a more recent treatment of the Presocratic cosmologists ("Plato and Presocratic Cosmology," 1964). In the last two essays ("Greek Philosophy and Modern Thought," 1978, and "Natural Science and the Concept of Nature," 1994/95) Gadamer puts these previous discussions into perspective for us by elaborating on the profound debt that modern scientific thinking owes to the Greek philosophical tradition. Just as in *The Beginning of Philosophy*, however, Plato continues to act as Gadamer's general point of entry into the Presocratic tradition. Not only does Plato provide the basic model for his project of bringing these various historical voices to language, but Gadamer recognizes that Plato's own appropriations of the Presocratics in the *Theaetetus*, the *Sophist*, and elsewhere, while typically overshadowed by those of Aristotle and subsequent the Hellenistic and Scholastic traditions, actually offer us the earliest intact accounts of these earliest of Western thinkers. This is not to say that we should simply adopt Plato's interpretations verbatim; but Gadamer's point is that we should never take the views of Aristotle, Simplicius, and Diogenes Laertius in this way either. In fact, from the causal agenda of Aristotle's own physics of substance to the religious agenda of Medieval Scholasticism, the Aristotelian tradition lays down so many layers of interpretation—often in the guise of direct quotation—that our view of the Presocratics has become extremely calcified and monolithic. According to Gadamer, Plato's renderings of the Presocratics, while certainly colored by their own philosophical perspective, offer us a pathway into these citations and fragments that can help us peel away and examine some of the layers of this philosophical and (as he reminds us) poetic palimpsest. For the key thing to understand when reading Gadamer on the Presocratics is that because he also reads the Platonic dialogues against the grain of the scientific tradition begun by Aristotle, and if by 'Presocratic' we mean before the advent of Platonism, Gadamer's Plato is himself something of a Presocratic thinker.

I would like to thank my editor at Continuum, Frank Oveis, for putting up with the seeming procrastinations of a community college professor whose teaching load often makes it difficult for him to meet translation deadlines. But I also want to thank my great friends Russell Winslow, for his draft of "Plato and Presocratic Cosmology," and Sigrid Koepke, without whose drafts of "Greek Philosophy and Modern Thought" and "Natural Science and the Concept of Nature" I might still be working on this book. However, as much as I appreciate their inestimable help in this endeavor, I myself assume sole responsibility for any and all errors and inconsistencies in the following translations.

Rod Coltman
Collin County Community College
June 2001

Author's Preface

Thanks to the work of Professor Vittorio De Cesare and Dr. Joachim Schulte, my 1988 Naples lectures (delivered in Italian and published in 1993 under the title, *L'inizio della filosofia occidentale*) have since appeared in German as *Der Anfang der Philosophie* (Reclam, 1997).[1]

We all know (or think we know) that the history of philosophy begins with Thales of Miletus, and we justifiably cite Aristotle (*Metaphysics* A) as our authority. And, thanks to Schleiermacher and Hegel, ever since the German Romantic period we have called these beginnings of philosophy 'Presocratic.' We know, however, that what has been handed down to us as the earliest philosophy are really only quotations or fragments of texts.

In my Naples lectures I wanted to show that we can only speak of this fragmented Presocratic tradition if we keep in mind the first philosophical texts that were actually received. These texts are mainly a question of the Platonic dialogues, on the one hand, and the enormous mass of Aristotle's writings, the *Corpus Aristotelicum*, on the other. Nevertheless, there is one exception among these fragments of the tradition, namely, the largely coherent text of the beginning of Parmenides' didactic poem. We owe this text to a reliable transcription by a great scholar from the last generation of ancient Greek scholars, an important member of the Academy in Athens by the name of Simplicius. He lived shortly before the dissolution of the Plato's Academy and left behind a series of commentaries, the most eminent of which were on Aristotle's *Physics*.

Centuries later, Athens is supposed to have fallen victim to the advance of Islam, at the hands of which even the eastern

---

1. [And these have since been translated into English and published as *The Beginning of Philosophy* (Continuum, 1999).]

Roman empire of Byzantium found its end. Nevertheless, this glorious locus of Greek thinking signified a very important point of release for the establishment of Italian humanism and the advent of the Renaissance. In truth, humanism and, above all, our tradition of Greek culture had their earliest beginnings in antiquity with the rise of Rome. After the victorious repulsion of the Punic threat, the circle of Scipio inaugurated a new direction for Roman society and a new education for its youth patterned on the Greek model. We need only recall the works of Cicero. In the time of the Caesars, Greek culture even experienced such a diffusion and consolidation of all things Greek that, generally speaking, one spoke Greek exclusively in the courts of the Roman Caesars. We owe this fact to that most brilliant thinker of this 'Hellenistic' epoch, Plotinus, whose students then successfully perpetuated this heritage for hundreds of years within an enduring Roman Empire. Above all, however, we owe the fact that Greek culture was transmitted to modernity to the later expansion of the Christian Church and the culture that developed from it through the disciplined work of the monks.

It is still fateful and decisive that only the first part, the introductory part, of Parmenides' didactic poem came to us along these paths. In reality, however, in his transcription of the text (which was found in Athens), Simplicius follows right along with the underlying fact that, in his *Physics*, Aristotle generally paid attention only to this introductory piece of the didactic poem, which is all that has survived. The entire text was composed in hexameters, the classic poetic language of Homer. The introductory verses of this earliest surviving piece show Parmenides the thinker to be a great writer who, through the mouth of a goddess, at once announces and grounds the great truth of being: the complete nothingness of the nothing. The far more extensive part of the didactic poem (which we do not have) gave evidence of contemporary cosmology and astronomy, but, like the individual fragments, it probably also dealt with the experience of the world that is disclosed to human beings. Apparently, to follow the instruction of the goddess would be to reject the nothingness of the nothing. She probably depicted the changing phenomena of nature with its wonderful rhythmic riddle of day and night, manifestation and obscurity. We can assume that the subsequent image of the world developed by Parmenides was surpassed in the mean time by the progress achieved by science, and this is why, from the perspectives of Plato and Aristotle, it was to be neglected.

Given that lectures tend to break off when time runs out, it is thus a happy coincidence that my little book on the beginning of philosophy—a book based on a series of Italian lectures—breaks off precisely at this point, with Parmenides.

Now, there was, however, another contemporary of Parmenides, from whom we admittedly possess no coherent text, but for whom we nevertheless possess an enormous wealth of profound quotations that were distributed widely in Hellenistic times in the form of a book. I am referring to Heraclitus, 'the dark one,' as he is often called in the tradition.

The question of how the two great contemporaries, Parmenides and Heraclitus, behaved toward each other has been debated in the scholarship for centuries. In the middle of the nineteenth century, philologists thought they had answered this question. According to them, Parmenides' didactic poem presented a response to the doctrine of flux in Heraclitean thinking, a doctrine which Parmenides critically rejected. Until relatively recently, this view has remained decisive for their ordering in the editions of the Presocratics. Karl Reinhardt's 1916 book changed the situation. Ever since then we no longer dare to assert any relationship at all between Parmenides and Heraclitus.

As the tradition makes unequivocally clear, Heraclitus came from an aristocratic family in Ephesus, a city on the coast of Asia Minor that, precisely at this period, was exposed to the pressure of the Persian expansion, which it would not withstand in the long run. Heraclitus is explicitly lauded for warning of the impending Persian invasion. We are really standing at a turning point in the cultural history of the entire West: we find ourselves in the so-called colonial period, a period in which, for example, the Greeks settled the southern Italian peninsula but, more importantly, a period that also impressed a Greek character upon Sicily and the coastal lands of the Mediterranean. To this period also belonged the reestablishment of Elea, where Parmenides lived and (thanks to the doctrine he received from Xenophanes) developed the 'school' that we call the Eleatic.

It is evident that the colonial expansion of Greece to the entire Mediterranean area and its particular concentration in Sicily and southern Italy was to be ascribed, above all, to the ever more strongly developing Persian pressure on the Aegean. A new upsurge of intellectual culture, particularly in Athens, began only after the victorious defense of the Greek mother country in the so-called Persian wars. We would certainly like to know how the intellectual development of the whole of Greek culture between the new colonial world and the mother country really took shape. But we learn nothing at all about it from Heraclitus.

The self-evident way in which scholars later posed the question of the relationship of the two thinkers is indeed strange. We only have to recall that Parmenides' didactic poem was written in hexameters, whereas the so-called book of Heraclitus, the exact beginning of which we happen to know because it is quoted in Aristotle, contains a wealth of profound and artful aphorisms and, in any case, offers a completely different prose style. They are not so much fragments as citations of famous and widely known epigrammatic sayings. Such sayings hardly constituted a coherent work of prose. One might rather suspect that the masterful execution of this style, which even we have to admire, is of a completely different origin from the epic art form of Homer and Hesiod. Whether it is at all meaningful to isolate thematic groups from out of the transmitted citations and to regard the whole as one prosaic text that we can understand, albeit in a fragmentary way, is extremely questionable. The most important objection to this is the fact that collections of aphorisms were part of the literature of the time, and they, too, exhibited thematic groupings. Uvo Hölscher in his essay, "Heraclitus between Tradition and Enlightenment,"[2] observed, no doubt correctly, that Heraclitus actually deposited his own manuscript in the temple of Ephesus and that he never, as was otherwise usual with authors, read his own text publicly. It is certainly also correct that Heraclitus never wished to be the founder of a school. We also detect in his writing style a new sort of rhetoric, one that was already intended for reading and not for recitation—a style that lent itself all the more to being quoted.

I daresay that the book known in Stoic times, much less the purported chapter divisions from the late Hellenistic period, can hardly date back to Heraclitus himself. Hölscher, like Kahn,[3] is nevertheless on the right path insofar as they both suspect in

2. *Antike und Abendland* 31.
3. Charles Kahn, *The Art and Thought of Heraclitus*, Cambridge 1979.

the tradition of Heraclitus less a competition between textbooks than a new form of literature. Both of their conclusions strengthen my conviction that Heraclitus is far younger than Xenophanes and Parmenides, the so-called Eleatics. In essence, of course, Heraclitus himself was a figure of the enlightenment, a thinker with no sophistic theatricality. Both authors see correctly what I have advocated for a long time: that Heraclitus' work did not belong in the lists of the cosmogonists and did not follow Hesiod. Was cosmology really of much interest to him at all, or was it, rather, the whole of human/political life? One wonders: Heraclitus has a new conception of *psychē* and *logos*, and even the poets know nothing like it. He is, after all, very much in search of himself.

Moreover, it is quite significant that Heraclitus is named and quoted with particular reverence in the Platonic dialogues, whereas Aristotle certainly appears familiar with Heraclitus, but derives nothing of particular interest from him. One can understand how Heraclitus' pointed way of writing might not be suited to Aristotle, the logician. In any case, the paradoxical mode of contradictory thinking that characterizes Heraclitus' aphorisms could be no great help for Aristotle's *Physics*.

We can clarify this with a specific example; I would like to use the concept of the soul, *psychē*, to illustrate the fact that the cosmological tradition of the Milesian school found itself greatly removed from Heraclitus' thinking. For the Milesians, the soul was the exhalation of the breath; for Heraclitus, on the other hand, the soul is the great mystery of the unfathomable limitlessness within which the thinking soul moves. Not just in the case Heraclitus, but also in comparable cases, the form of the *gnōmē*, the aphorism, is stamped with a peculiar basic attitude. Anyone who quotes Heraclitus does not have cosmology in mind. Once the later, victorious Empedoclean doctrine of the four elements underlies the style of Aristotle, one has a very hard time with fire. With his ingenious hypothesis about the stars, Anaximander had already explained the consuming and uncontainable destructive force of fire by means of holes in the firmament. But just as the soul in Heraclitus indicates a new dimension of interiority, wherever there is heat, according to Heraclitus, there is fire; thus there is not just fire in the heavens but everywhere—wherever the heat of life is. Also, we should not be so ready, as philology has been until recently, to push aside the

later report, the one in which Heraclitus' book had nothing at all
to do with nature but rather with the *polis* and politics. We can
tell from this example how in the development of the Presocratic
tradition Aristotle's *Physics* has insinuated itself again and again
into the conduct of the scholarship.

We will have to ask ourselves how, not just Heraclitus but
Parmenides as well, both perform their functions in facilitating
the beginnings of Greek philosophizing. To that end, let us
investigate the work of these two. The Platonic dialogue, *Parmenides*, gives us a clear reference. It is Zeno who opens the
conversation with the young Socrates at this point and thereby
clears a path to the mathematical groundwork of the Pythagoreans. One anticipates how the theory of atoms will announce
itself in the end. Indeed, they keep strictly to the nothingness
of the nothing and the unchangeability of being; for all appearances and effects move the unchangeable atoms. The true being
of Parmenides, about which the goddess teaches him, is thus
confirmed in the end in the multiplicity of its appearances. In this
kind of corpuscular theory, neither originating nor passing away
is burdened with the non-thought of nothingness. The massive
counter-thesis that one sees as the genuine truth in Heraclitus
seems more difficult—the thesis that everything changes constantly and that the one world has its true being in this stream in
which everything flows. We can nevertheless imagine that the true
being of Parmenides and his goddess is confirmed by the mystery
of death and birth, which eludes all attempts to think it. Admittedly, in reading the Heraclitean sayings we certainly cannot
follow him into the darkness every time, but we always detect the
deep mystery of the one, the mystery of the one/being.[4]

It is not without reason that I preface a work on the tradition
of Heraclitus with a consideration of Heraclitus' style. In a striking way, it seems to me to confirm that opposites belong together
irresolvably. Three hundred years after Christ (prior to the predominance of the idea of the sameness of what is different),
Hippolytus dares a bold anachronism on the basis of his Christian heritage that is supposed to serve the understanding of the
mystery of the Trinity. I believe I have shown that, for application to the Trinity, Hippolytus proceeded from such a simple
truth as Heraclitus' idea that the father who begets a son makes

4. [*das Geheimnis des Eins-Seins*]

himself into the father at the same time. When plugged into dialectical epigrammatic sayings, these become intellectual temptations. They offer themselves again and again as formulas for particular possibilities. We might not, therefore, be so surprised to find the inclusion of atomic theory. What is new and essential is that it is the language itself that indicates the unity of opposites. We detect how a new sovereign domain is opened up here for the *logos*, one that does not allow itself to be portrayed in hexameters. Zeno is presented in the *Parmenides* as someone who cannot separate himself from the one that Parmenides insists upon. Socrates' insistence on the *eidos*, the idea, is seen no differently, as if, by the exclusion of the many, the one of being would retain its meaning without the many. The famous Zenonian paradoxes are the classic example of this self-fulfilling prophecy.

It is like a new imperative to recognize and hold fast to the unity in that which changes itself. This turns all of the Heraclitean propositions into one truth of unfathomable depth. We can understand that the power of the *logos* has always already comprehended what is contradictory as a unity, which means, that, precisely in the differentiation of occurrences, not change but abiding being justifies its application to Heraclitus and a distinction as Heraclitean—just as the truth of the ideas is articulated in Plato's *Theaetetus* and taught in the *Sophist*.

A lecture held before the *Accademia dei Lincei* in Rome forms the conclusion of this volume. It is our task to point out again and again that our scientific culture owes its proficiency to the vigilant accompaniment of the enlightenment and—in a great arc from the beginning of philosophy on—to be reminded again and again of the limits that are placed on the knowledge and ability of humanity. It is the arc from the atomic theory of Democritus past Galileo up to the limiting experiences of our knowledge and its application.

Hans-Georg Gadamer
Heidelberg 1998

1
On the Tradition
of Heraclitus

Hegel, the man who was convinced that there was not a single idea in Heraclitus' propositions that he had not absorbed into his own logic, was not alone in being profoundly drawn to Heraclitus. Indeed, the oracle-like paradoxes handed down from Heraclitus hold a special fascination. Variations on one and the same idea, variations on the ideas of the One and the Same, which, in their difference, their tension, their oppositionality, their consequences, and their change, are the sole true thing— the *logos* of Heraclitus: these appear as the oracular utterances of what Hegel, at the end of the Western metaphysical tradition, called 'the speculative.' Ever since then, the nearness of Heraclitus is felt wherever philosophical questions are set into motion. Anyone who has ever been a guest in Heidegger's hut in Todtnauberg recalls the saying scratched into a piece of bark and placed above the lintel: *ta de panta oiakizei keraunos*; "Lightning steers all" (Fragment 64). These words are like an oracular pronouncement and a paradox at the same time. For, surely, this saying does not refer to that attribute of the lord of the heavens with which he thunders his decisions down to earth, but rather the abrupt lightning-filled elucidation that makes everything visible in one stroke, yet in such a way that the darkness immediately engulfs it again. In any event, this may be how Heidegger tied his own questions back into Heraclitus' profundity. For, to Heidegger, the dark task of his thinking was not, as it was for Hegel, the omnipresence of the self-knowing spirit that unites within it sameness in change and the speculative unity of opposites, but precisely that insoluble unity and duality of revealing and concealing, light and darkness, into which human thinking finds itself interpolated. It lights up in this flash, which most certainly did not, as Hippolytus thought it did, represent the 'eternal fire.'

Those of us who owe the movement of our own attempts at thinking to the stimulus of Heidegger's thought are overcome by the same fascination emanating from Heraclitus and in the same sense. The words of Heraclitus, which, as Socrates put it, require a Delian diver to lift them from the dark depths to the light (Diogenes Laertius II, 22), stand in a curious tension with the employment of his words by later figures. At best, one can still trace in Plato something of the well-honed sharpness of Heraclitus' thinking and the compactness of his propositions— as in the *Sophist* (242a), where Plato explicitly refers to the Ionic muses of Heraclitus as being more tension-filled than the Sicilian ones of Empedocles and thus recognizes in Heraclitus' words the enactment of the one and the many, of separation and union, which poses the task for his own dialectic. Nevertheless, the doxographical tradition that begins with Aristotle has read Heraclitus' doctrine back into the context of the older physiologists, and many testimonies are cited to the effect that Heraclitus also endorsed the great cosmic order of beings that Aristotle's interpretation of *physis* understood as the start of Greek thinking. Now, there are many other sayings handed down under the name of Heraclitus that adapt themselves more readily to a moralistic tradition. The cosmology of fire, which can be reconstructed from Aristotle, is badly suited to this. This is why antiquity had already doubted whether Heraclitus' writings dealt with nature at all and not rather with the *politeia*.[1] But it seems to be his special distinction that he could be called to testify for the most diverse interests. However, the peculiar difficulty

---

1. The grammarian, Diodotus, says plainly: *ta de peri phuseôs en paradeigmatos eidei keisdai* (Diels 142, 30). [The abbreviation DK (followed by volume and page numbers) will be used hereafter to refer to specific pages in the three-volume edition of *Die Fragmente der Vorsokratiker*, edited by Hermann Diels and Walther Kranz. The abbreviation VS will be used to designate chapter numbers for the list of Presocratic citations themselves within Diels/Kranz.]

that Heraclitus interpretation holds for us also has its roots in this. From the technical-hermeneutical standpoint, this is a true textbook example of how few unambiguous points of access such texts offer for understanding and that nothing is so untrustworthy as a quotation ripped out of its context. As is well known, Heraclitus' doctrine of fire has precipitated a long effective history stretching all the way from Stoic pneumatology to the Christian eschatological ideas of global conflagration and hell-fires. Meanwhile, this doctrine has been further elucidated, and by Karl Reinhardt in particular. According to the model of such philologists as Karl Reinhardt, it is apparently necessary to first take the literal-sounding Heraclitus citations that we encounter back into the context of the quoting author and then, based on his interests, determine the meaning he intended. Only then can a second step succeed, which traces the faults, breaks, splits, and incongruities that sometimes open up within the Heraclitus citation and against the sense intended by the quoting author.

These undertakings would be hopeless if we did not have numerous sayings from Heraclitus that have apparently been preserved word for word precisely because of the distinctive peculiarity of their diction. His style was renowned. He seems to have had hardly any literary models. At best we encounter a comparable tension and clear definition of expression in the choral odes of tragedy, which are fond of the dialectical *contrapposto*[2] as a poetic parallel to the dance steps of the chorus. But here in Heraclitus we find a notoriously sententious prose, the greatest mystery of which was its dearth of words. Perhaps we can glimpse a certain initial stage of his style of thought and speech in the few Anaximander fragments that we possess and which even attracted the attention of Theophrastus as being particularly ceremonious (Diels A 9). In any case, we have to proceed from a negative criterion: wherever Heraclitus speaks plainly and clearly—and it has been occasionally alleged that he can do this—what is most peculiar to him will barely come

2. [A stance of the human body in which one leg bears the weight, while the other is relaxed, creating an asymmetry in the hip-shoulder axis. Sometimes referred to as "counterpoise," it stems from the difference between the stiff pose of the archaic Greek *kouros* and the more natural pose of the classical Greek figure.]

to language or, at least, is no longer recognizable. For it can hardly be doubted that some of the sayings attributed to him owe their provocative triviality merely to the fact that we do not know the context from which they presumably received their gist. Would Heraclitus, thirty miles from Miletus, really have proposed the doctrine that the sun is a the size of a foot (Fragment 3)? Whether another received saying (i.e., Fragment 45) can be associated so trivially with a punch line, as, for instance, Hermann Fraenkel tried to do, it is hard to say. But there is more to it. Many a received saying has within it a hidden harmony that is more striking than the obvious one. We can legitimately take such sayings as the standard. All these considerations should only serve to justify why it is a methodologically allowable undertaking to read Heraclitus citations against the meaning that the quoting author lends them and reduce them to a tenseness of form that eliminates the editing of the quoting author. This has already happened successfully in some cases; but experts in the tradition, like Karl Reinhardt, have pointed out repeatedly that, given the inaccurate mode of reference and quotation that was common in later antiquity, many a Heraclitus saying may still drift unrecognized in the misty waters of the Christian apologists.

It is all the more astonishing, however, that even to this day sayings handed down under the name of Heraclitus have not always attracted the proper attention and effort needed to distill from them the thoughts and wording of Heraclitus himself. So, I would like to dedicate this small contribution to an attempt at salvaging a new fragment from Hippolytus, one that the collections have missed until now—not that it would have remained unknown. For the long list of Heraclitus citations that Hippolytus places together in his ninth book and subjects to his apologetical intent explicitly distinguishes all the quoted sayings as putatively Heraclitean. In the introduction to this collection of citations (which we read as Fragment 50 in Diels) a series of oppositional pairs is recounted, presumably to which the subsequent quotations should then correspond. Even 'father-son' occurs among these oppositional pairs. At this point in Diels, the list is already regarded as a Christian addition. But a (purported) Heraclitus saying declaring the unity of father and son actually occurs as the last quotation in the series; it thus corresponds to a kind of initial stage of the Incarnation dogma. *Hote men oun mê gegenêto*

*ho patêr, dikaiôs patêr prosêgoreuto, hote de êudokêsen genesin
hupomeinai, gennêtheis ho huios egeneto autos heautou, ouch
heterou.* "So long as the father did not come into being, can he
rightly be named father. However, when he condescended to
take becoming upon himself, he became the son of himself and
not of someone else." So, supposedly what the heretic Noetus
teaches is already in the heathen Heraclitus. It is clear that the
sense of this sentence is 'Christian,' but it is also clear even from
the wording, that a phrase like, "when he condescended to take
becoming upon himself," could never be Heraclitus'. Even the
understanding of the word 'becoming' in this text is that of a
Christian Platonism. It is therefore understandable that the collections of Heraclitus citations have not taken this quotation
into account. What is Heraclitean about it? And yet, our quoting
author seems very sure of his subject matter when he says: "Yet
everyone knows that, according to Heraclitus, father and son are
the same." From where does everyone know this? Evidently
only from the purported Heraclitus citation that follows at that
point. Is this pure fiction, or, as in the previous series of quotations, is there a real Heraclitus saying at the bottom of it, one that
expresses this unity—though surely in a completely different
sense? I think we have to consider this seriously. Should it not be
possible, even in this sentence, to strip away the Christian veneer
and recover the words of Heraclitus?

As always with hermeneutical problems of this sort, one
must follow the first essential pieces of evidence that present
themselves. In this way, I have even had something like a modest inspiration concerning this quotation at two points: the problematic issue of the relationship of father and son and the extreme
brachiology of 'the son of himself.' Quite apart from the question
of whether there is anything Christian here or not, if we were to
consider what the sameness of father and son could mean at
all, the first thing that occurred to us for Heraclitus would probably not be the unity of family and blood. For the genealogical
unity of father and son as it underlies the aristocratic model
of ethics and education or even the political unity of a ruling
dynasty whose autocracy does not restrict itself to the succession
of the son (as Noetus apparently understood it) is surely not
what is meant by that great loner, Heraclitus, the man who
claims to place himself, along with his doctrine, over against
all other human beings. Whatever is to be rightly attributed to his

name must already be something unexpected. Indeed, in this case the relationship of father and son lends itself to a curious alternative determination. The father really only becomes a father when he becomes the father of his son. Could there be something like this behind the quotation by Hippolytus?

The use of the word 'becoming' in the received passage certainly carries unmistakably Platonic overtones. But perhaps this Platonic use of the word was developed from a text that occurs in a completely different context, one in which *genesthai* and *gennasthai*, becoming and having been born, are still one and the same. Indeed, we also say that one becomes a father, and this is also what it means in Hippolytus in a different context (VI, 29): *hina genêtai patêr*. But, the fact that one becomes a father is at the same time the consequence of one's own action. What 'becomes' here is evidently not just that the generating father generates the son (*ho gennêsas patêr*, in the language of Homer). Rather, he only generates himself as father in thus generating the son. Surprisingly, this does occur in the text when we reduce it to its elements: *dikaiôs patêr prosêgoreuto… gennêseis*, which means: 'a father can justifiably be called generated'—or even: 'a father can justifiably be addressed as a father when he has become it.' If this is supposed to be the gist of the sentence, then we can also understand quite well the idea of the final clause, the idea that, in this instance, one would be generated by oneself (and not, as is added explanatorily, by someone else). The father who makes himself a father is, so to speak, his own son. And this occurs again in the text with *ho huios egeneto autos heautou*, which means: 'the son of himself.' This statement implies not only the inseparability of being father and being son, as is natural to all relational concepts, but also the sameness of becoming father and becoming son. This corresponds very well to otherwise familiar Heraclitean oppositions behind which the unity of the occurrence has to be thought. It also shows, it seems to me, the full terseness of the Heraclitean tone. I would therefore suspect this to be the Heraclitean wording: *dikaiôs patêr prosêgoreuto gennêtheis huios heautou*, 'One is only rightly then called father when one has become one' (and this does not just mean that he is the generator); 'the son of himself' (and not that of another). Both sets of parentheses are merely explications, which I only added in order to accentuate how paradoxical it is to read *gennêtheis* expressed by him instead of *ho gennêsas patêr*, the other additions serving the same purpose in the traditional text of Hippolytus.

We can put forward for this reconstruction the idea that one could understand how a 'Christian' Platonist like Noetus or Hippolytus (who were, of course, very well acquainted not only with the Platonic concept of *genesis* but also with the dialectic of the relational concepts) exploited this well-honed formulation of Heraclitus' as an anticipation of the Christian unity of Father and Son. If my reconstruction is correct, Hippolytus apparently connects Noetus' 'monarchism' to *huios autos heautou* and thereby to the clever paradox of the unity of becoming father and becoming son with which Heraclitus carried on his dialectical game. Incidentally, this line of argumentation is also handed down with Hippolytus outside of all relationship to Heraclitus and belongs to the ambivalent Trinity speculation of the early Church Fathers. In the long Simon citation (VI, 18), it is called: *phaneis de autôi apo heautou, egeneto deuteros. All' oude patêr eklêthê prin autên auton onomasai patêra.* Certainly no one would suspect Heraclitus here. But in our passage there is no question of guessing. The text is handed down as the words of Heraclitus, and the only methodical way of rehabilitating it is to look for its Heraclitean gist. After all, the Simon parallel shows us how the alternate edition of the hypothetical Heraclitus passage (predicated on Noetus' monarchism) was, as it were, in the air. Apparently, even the introduction to the *polemos* fragment (page 53) alludes to this paradox. At this point in Hippolytus the father of all that has come into being is called *genêtos agenêtos, ktisis dêmiourgos*: the second phrase is directed toward the Creation, the first is directed toward the Trinity (or half of it). But the first phrase cannot be inferred at all from the subsequent Heraclitus citation as such: that the one proves himself to be the father and the other to be the son should come about through war! So we can see that having the sameness of father and son constantly in mind suspends Hippolytus from his dogmatic bias against Noetus, and thus we are again led indirectly to the Heraclitean background of the passage we analyzed above. Indeed, a very different original color has been exposed from behind the Christian veneer: the unity of generating and becoming generated. This is entirely in keeping with the style of Hippolytus' lecture on the doctrines of Heraclitus. Hippolytus wants to show, by using Heraclitus, that

Noetus has wrongly claimed the sameness of father and son to be Christian. The quotation is therefore polemically motivated. But this is precisely why it is hardly a pure fabrication. On the other hand, we need not be surprised at the total capriciousness of Hippolytus, through whom (in my reconstruction) Heraclitus becomes stylized into a pseudo-Christian and monarchistic heretic.

In the same Hippolytus text we once again meet a similarly palpable Christian veneer. Fragment 63 relates a passage to the Resurrection, a passage which again is unequivocally attributed to Heraclitus. The Diels-Kranz translation reads (admittedly remaining quite uncertain in view of the circumstances of the transmission): "Before him, who is there, however, they would arise and become watchers of the living and the dead." (In the same context—as a prior reference to the world's trial by fire— follows the beautiful proposition, "Lightning steers all.") Even in this Fragment 63, it does not seem to me all that difficult to clear away the Christian veneer. Karl Reinhardt created a good presupposition for this in that he recognized the doctrine of *ekpyrosis* as Stoic/Christian and therefore discarded such statements as Fragment 66: "For fire will have approached everything, judging and seizing." He capitulated, however, before the above-cited Heraclitus passage in Fragment 63. I would like to attempt an interpretation by placing myself in the conceptual world of Heraclitus. There we find sufficient evidence, as in Fragments 24 and 25, for instance (but compare 29 also), that the death of the hero in battle and the exaltation of the fallen in the glory and memory of the people has a bearing on this. We will not assume that Heraclitus attempted to subordinate himself to the goals of a political admonition. Rather, the 'one lone wise thing' must also stand behind whatever it was in heroic death and hero worship that set him thinking. I believe it is what is sudden and unpredictable in the changing of things that occupies him: as death in battle leads to the exaltation and glorification of the fallen and allows death to appear as a higher form of life. Of course, it is likewise said of war that it 'proves' one man to be a god and another a human being. It seems to me that such exaltation (in the most literal sense) occurs in our text in the Greek phrase, *epaniotasthai*, 'raises itself.' In such a context, the idea that one turns into the watcher who watches takes on the meaning that the fallen one, like a caretaker of the just, places all virtue and glory before the eyes of the others. Perhaps even the

Christian sounding phrase 'over the living and the dead' has a genuine original sense here: these icons of bravery stand erected for the survivors, just as they do for all of the dead upon whom no fame attends. The Christian echo of Christ's journey to Hell and his reign over the living and the dead could thus be quite supplementary—just as supplementary and surely as unwarranted as the identification in the subsequent lines of lightning with eternal fire.

It used to be that if one wanted once again to scrutinize the procedures of the mystery cults in great detail—as Diels does at Fragment 63 as well as at Fragment 26—the fact that Heraclitus, positioning himself as the outsider, clearly criticized all such strange cult-practices (Fragment 51) would, in principle, speak against such an examination. That his language may remind us of the mystery cults need not be disputed. But it goes without saying that the man who ordained himself as the sole initiate into the *hen sophon* could not equate himself with the initiates of a cult community. In fact, unambiguous evidence teaches us that he posits himself as the outsider with respect to the religions no less sharply than he does with respect to the so-called sages.

It has already been mentioned that Heraclitus' doctrine of fire—much like the unity of father and son and the (supposed) resurrection—found a Christian resonance that was, in this case, Stoically mediated. Here, too, a stripping away of the Christian veneer seems possible to me, and one should be wary of completely rejecting any saying attributed to Heraclitus in this list of Hippolytus' citations. Reinhardt has made it plausible that Heraclitus himself may have called fire *phronimon*, meaning 'reasonable.' The idea that fire goes together with brightness, dryness, fineness, facility, and thus, in the end, with insight, also resonates with other parts of Heraclitus. Thus, we must look for a connection between fire and the profound things that Heraclitus says about the *psychê*. In any case, we always have to consider to what extent an original Heraclitean meaning can be guessed at behind the Christian veneer. The statement, *panta gar to pur epelthon krinei kai katalêpsetai*, "fire will judge and apprehend all things," is of this sort. This could actually be seen as a rational expression by Heraclitus if we were to translate *krinein* not with 'to judge' but rather with 'to separate' and we meant by this only that fire is capable of seizing all that is combustible to burn and of making everything thing else glow.[3] Indeed, this would not simply be a bad allusion to the cosmological problem that fire is supposed to be an elementary component of the world order. To think of the devouring flame that consumes everything and which nothing resists as a part of the existing order of the universe is evidently a particular problem for ancient cosmology. Even Timaeus, the Pythagorean, finds himself led toward the subtle application of a double parallel in order to hold fire and water apart in the distribution of the elements so that the world *philian eschen* (*Timaeus* 32 b). For Heraclitus, the peculiarity of fire apparently lies in the irresistible force with which it is able to seize everything—and yet, it is "kindling according to measure and going out according to measure." A world order is not possible without there being limits placed even on fire—as by the arc of the sun's course.

What is it, however, that allows the consuming fire to rise to such a level of expressive value that it can oppose the Milesian cosmological idea of balance with provocative decisiveness (Fragment 31)? The Milesians taught the transition of air, water, and earth into one another, hence the change of aggregate states, but they certainly did not include fire in this balancing process (as Fragment 30 does). On the contrary, we see what cosmological trouble Anaximander has connecting the fire of heaven with the world order—in spite the consuming spread that is peculiar to fire. He invents that dividing valence with apertures through which the glow of fire shines in the gentle arc of warming or illuminating heavenly bodies (Diels A 12). Heraclitus, on the other hand, dares to single out fire—that which lives forever—straightforwardly as the One behind all appearances and

3. This is how the Sextus commentary worked out the effectiveness of the *theios logos* in Heraclitus: *diapuroi ginontai phôristhentes de sbennuntai* (VS A 16, 130). See Empiricus B 62, 2: *krinomenon pur*; in any case, 'the self-separating fire' (Diels) at that point, is also a fire that gives the impulse for the *diakrinesthai* of the things (*Met.* A 4 985 a 24). For Heraclitus, the juridical sense, which naturally deceived the Church Father, suggests itself neither for *krinein* nor for *katalambanesthai*. (One also compares Hippasos [VS 8 A 11], where, next to *pur* and *psychê ho arithmos* appears as *kritikon kosmourgou theou organon*.) On the contrary, the sentence is not a deleterious commentary on *haptesthai* (Fragment 26), which fascinated Heraclitus as a phenomenon just as it did as a metaphor, as I demonstrate in what follows.

transitions. This is certainly less 'cosmology' than it is critique. Underlying this is an interest in viewing *psychê* and 'thinking' together with fire. This can be illustrated in two ways. First, in the Heraclitean unity of flowing and standing still that the consuming light (the oil lamp) and its standing flame lock up so well within themselves like the sameness of the soul, which steams up from out of the moisture (Fragment 12). Then, up to the highest condition: "The human being strikes a light in the night, entirely from out of himself" (Fragment 26).

According to this, the doctrine of flux and the doctrine of the soul seem to belong together in the most intimate way. I do not want to treat the obscure Fragment 26[4] here in its entirety; rather, I would only like to point out that the stylistic reconstruction of this sentence seems to me still very much lacking. As verbose as this proposition sounds, Heraclitus certainly was not. I therefore consider both instances of *'aposbestheis opseis'*[5] in this fragment to be later explanatory additions, and I wonder whether Heraclitus did not also expect that when he said 'life' we would understand 'death' at the same time?[6] But it is yet another side of this connection that makes fire's 'cosmological' distinction comprehensible. Heraclitus certainly saw fire and heat as one and the same in principle (as did Plato). It is fire that is in us and everything that has heat. The open outbreak of fire is something quite different only with regard to appearances—and only in the eyes of laymen. This is how Heraclitus must have thought of it. If this is correct, then a way to make the two-sidedness of heat fire and flame fire on the one hand and of life and consciousness on the other a little more understandable seems to suggest itself to me, and once again so that a reference to Heraclitus imposes itself at an unexpected place. It is a passage in Plato's *Charmides* (168e ff.). The question of the self-relatedness of knowledge is discernable there: "Hearing and seeing as well as the movement that moves itself... and all such things may admittedly have much that is implausible, yet perhaps not for some,

---

4. [The entire fragment reads, "A man strikes a light for himself in the night, when his sight is quenched. Living, he touches the dead in his sleep; waking, he touches the sleeper" (Kahn 70).]

5. ["when his sight quenched" or, perhaps, "extinguished."]

6. So that *apothanon* by itself would be the only explanatory addition (as Wilamowitz had already assumed).

even if it requires a great man to distinguish that this movement has its *dynamis* within itself." The context of this sentence aims at the paradox of a knowledge that knows nothing
but itself. As a rule, relatedness is always directed toward something else—for example, the bigger toward the smaller (168c).
But seeing and hearing also clearly have something like a relation
back to themselves, just as when Aristotle says (with regard to
seeing and hearing) that there is a perception of the perception
(*De Anima* III 2). As an initial stage of the knowledge of knowledge, therefore, these two examples are quite pertinent. It is
much the same with self-movement, which is indeed the secret of
life, the *psychê*. In fact, this is how Plato (in the *Phaedrus* and in
Book 10 of the *Laws*) taught this self-relatedness of the *psychê*,
that is, the movement that moves itself—this is also a good connecting link between vision, hearing, and knowledge. But in
this list—in among the senses and self-movement and, ultimately, the knowledge of knowledge—there now conspicuously
stands what I omitted from the text: *kai thermotês kaein*,
'the heat that kindles.' Heat, here, seems to have invoked a kind
of self-movement or spontaneous combustion. The phenomenon being described here is clearly the sudden flaring up of
flames from the heated log. This stands here between the self-
movement of what is living and the self-relatedness of knowledge.
Now, it also seems to me that this position is not entirely
insignificant. What is astounding about this phenomenon is its
lack of transition. In the light having been ignited everything
has all of a sudden become completely different (Fragment 26:
haptesthai), as in the appearance of lightning, as in the brightness
of self-igniting thought. It was surely not a natural scientific
interest that Heraclitus took in the idea of kindling—probably no
more than it was an interest in 'the transformations of fire'
(Fragment 31); it was the incomprehensibility of the media-
tionless transition that sets him thinking about this as well as
about 'the one.' The transitionlessness of this transition from
sleep to wakefulness or from life to death ultimately points
toward the enigmatic experience of thinking, which suddenly
awakens and then sinks again completely into darkness.

2

Heraclitus Studies

Heraclitus remains a constant challenge for every kind of thinking. Men like Hegel, Nietzsche, and Heidegger meet this challenge in fundamentally different ways. Countless pages of philological commentary on Heraclitus have been produced. But what was valid for antiquity still seems valid today. He is still the dark one. There is no single reliable fundamental perspective that allows us to grasp this figure shimmering between moralisms and metaphysics. Nevertheless, it seems to me that two points have not been sufficiently considered—the way that Plato is related to Heraclitus and the style in which Heraclitus constructs his propositions.

At the outset I will delineate the philosophical significance associated with every Heraclitus interpretation, and then I will enter into the hermeneutical problem, often in a philological way. What we possess of Heraclitus are isolated citations from later authors, beginning with Plato and running through the whole of later antiquity. In addition to these later citations, with Heraclitus there is also the question of the aphoristic propositions that were already famous in antiquity because of their darkness and their profundity. Socrates is supposed to have said that what he understood of them was splendid. He trusted, therefore, that the many propositions that he had not understood were equally splendid. Admittedly, it would take a Delian diver—a master diver—to bring this treasure from out of the depths toward the light.[1]

---

1. VS 22 A 4. Fragment numbers indicated in the Heraclitus citations

But there is yet another enormous difficulty that constantly diverts us in all our philosophical understandings of Greek thinking, and it is operative in the case of Heraclitus as well. It is the ongoing effect of the institution of modern science, the pioneering act of which was Galilean physics and which dominates all of our habitual modes of thought. Ever since Galileo, the concept of method has been deemed to be constitutive of what can be called science. This is connected with the fact that the philosophy of modernity has erected its philosophical self-grounding upon the concept of self-consciousness. As a rule, we look to Descartes' famous meditation on doubt for the turning point that is established with the development of the modern natural sciences. There, the 'cogito ergo sum' was singled out as the indubitable reality of whatever thinks and doubts and as the surest and most unshakeable fundament of all certainty. To be sure, this was not yet a philosophy of reflection in the full sense of the word, a philosophy grounded in the concept of the subject and from out of which a new sense of objectivity redefines itself. But ever since Kant took up the Cartesian distinction of the 'res cogitans' in the critical demonstration of his transcendental philosophy and grounded the justification of the concepts of the understanding upon the synthesis of apperception, upon the fact that the 'I think' must be able to accompany all of my ideas, the concept of subjectivity has been elevated to a central position. Developing this as a program, the followers of Kant (especially Fichte) derive all justification for truth, all grounding for validity in general, from the principle of self-consciousness. Thus the primacy of self-consciousness, as opposed to the 'consciousness of something,' became the stigma of modern thinking. Even Husserl's ambitious attempt to develop philosophy, for the first time, into a strict science remained firmly rooted in this soil, the soil from which the bold thought experiments of Heidegger and Wittgenstein sought to free themselves. By that time, in fact, German Idealism had already formulated something that characterized, in philosophically appropriate terms, the new place of humanity in the world: the aggressive attitude of modern science toward the nature that surrounds us. Subjectivity,

in this text reflect the numbering in DK. But always compare to I. Bywater (*Heracliti Ephesii Reliquiae*, Oxford 1877) and Charles H. Kahn (*The Art and Thought of Heraclitus*, Cambridge 1979).

in the form of transcendental philosophy, has accompanied the triumphal march of science. Meanwhile, doubts about the certainty of self-consciousness have taken hold of modern science and kept it in suspense. It began with Nietzsche. The psychologist in Nietzsche issued the following challenge regarding Descartes' meditation on doubt: "It must be doubted even more fundamentally." This fulfilled itself in the radical unnerving of naive self-certainty and led to such doubts about the assertion of self-consciousness as we are confronted with from the most divergent of perspectives—from historicism, from the critique of ideology, or from psychoanalysis. Ever since Nietzsche, constantly rethinking the problematic central role that self-consciousness plays in philosophy has become an unavoidable task.

We can be led into this question by the phenomenological evidence that Franz Brentano first reproduced and that Aristotle had not been altogether unaware of in his 'anthropology' (*De Anima* Γ) or even in his grounding of 'first philosophy' upon the self-thinking *nous*. Over against the intentionality of a consciousness that is always consciousness of something, the reflexivity of self-consciousness holds a secondary status. The primacy of self-consciousness can only be maintained if we grant an absolute priority to the ideal of certainty, or better yet, to the ideal of methodologically confirming the validity of mathematical construction with respect to reality, as it has constituted the essence of the modern natural sciences ever since Galileo.

Even though (as the 'primum movens' and as constant self-presence) it is the highest of beings, the god of Aristotelian ontotheology in no way functions as grounding or securing human knowledge. The structure of selfhood points toward contexts other than that 'fundamentum inconcussum' by which self-consciousness holds firm against all scepticism. If anything can truly come to the aid of our modern reflection on the riddle of self-consciousness, it is probably the fact that the Greeks possessed neither an expression for the subject or subjectivity nor an expression for consciousness and the concept of the I. Even though they ultimately took that which shows itself into consideration along with the wonder of thinking itself, the Greeks (including Aristotle) did not assert a central position for self-consciousness.

In order to be freed from this modernistic perspective, we find ourselves directed back into the historical dimension that leads from Descartes to Augustine, from Augustine to Plato. Now I would like to show that, from Plato, it must be traced back even further—to Heraclitus.

The question poses itself as to whether we may view Heraclitus from this problem-context of self-consciousness at all, or whether his thinking does not direct us along a different path instead, that is, toward the place of human beings in the world. Heraclitus enjoys a special fame. He owes this fame not just to his above-mentioned proverbial darkness and not just to the use to which Plato had already put his name, and, ultimately, not to his presence in Hegel, who, at the end of the entire thought-path of Western metaphysics said that there was not a single proposition in Heraclitus that he could not take up into his own logic. Moreover, Heraclitus' thinking exerted a peculiar attraction for Nietzsche's radical extremism as well as for Heidegger's insight into the end and the beginning of metaphysics. At one time, anyone who had been in Heidegger's hut in Todtnauberg, high in the Black Forest, would have seen, carved into a piece of bark above the front door, the Heraclitean statement, "Lightning steers all,"[2] a strange and deeply moving statement—and an apparent paradox. In place of the steady hand that steers the ship through the waves, we find the lightning that flashes suddenly and then goes out. We can puzzle over the meaning of this statement, but the interpretation that prevails to this day, that of seeing the lighting as the attribute of an all-steering godhead, fails to hear the paradox that should definitely be attended to in Heraclitus. Of course, the particular fascination that emanates from Heraclitus does not ultimately depend upon the paradoxes and dialectical structure of such statements. The speculative tension of his thinking leads him again and again to the most extreme and finely honed formulations. All of these formulations are like the proposition concerning the ever-flowing river that is never the same when we step into it—and up out of which the soul steams (Fragment 12).

Now, of course, as modern scholars bred to historical critique, we cannot immediately get ourselves involved in a naive identification with the mythic power of such statements. We must concentrate on the respective conditions of the tradition, the conditions that offer us access to the texts, which we are

2. Fragment 64: *ta de panta oiakizei keraunos.*

reading as fragments. Meanwhile, we know all too well what quotations are, what we can do with quotations, how we can misuse quotations, their meanings being hidden to the point of indecipherability. Heraclitus scholarship is thus a special kind of hermeneutical task. We must constantly ask ourselves: How does one uncover, how does one excavate what is suggested to us by the quoting authors in their prior understandings, and with which methods can we reach a historically appropriate and nevertheless philosophically meaningful understanding of Heraclitus and his statements?

From the outset, I think, a certain priority can now be claimed for our oldest witness, and that is Plato. His writings are the very first philosophical texts that we possess in their entirety. Everything earlier is fragments, that is, citations or collections of citations from later writers who no doubt still knew Heraclitus' book, but who enlisted it precisely for their own purposes. Plato, of course, also did this in that he orchestrated his own thinking with his references to Heraclitus. But he remains our oldest witness.

The Platonic dialogues yield a particularly ambivalent picture of Heraclitus. On the one hand, Heraclitus is employed as the originator and symbol of a worldview which knows nothing of the abiding sameness of the essence of things, of the 'eidos,' but instead sees everything in change, everything in flux. In one famous construct in the *Theaetetus* (152e), Plato characterizes all previous thinkers from Homer to Protagoras (with the single exception of Parmenides) as Heraclitean. For anyone familiar with the Platonic mode, this means that Heraclitus is stylized here as a type, a type that does not necessarily concur with what Plato himself had seen in Heraclitus—or even what Heraclitus actually said and intended. It is amazing how Plato clumps everyone together here as Heraclitean! Here, Heraclitus simply presents a kind of counter-type. Whatever is placed under his name should point emphatically toward the exception, which, in Plato's eyes, presents the great Eleatic as the precursor of Plato's own thinking of the *eidos*.

If we keep in mind the other references to Heraclitus in the Platonic corpus, however, all of a sudden the situation appears entirely different. In a famous passage from the *Sophist* (242c ff.), to which we must look for the roots of all our scholarly knowledge of Presocratic doctrines, it is said of the earlier ones that while one taught that the many was what truly existed another taught just the contrary—that it was the one. But the Ionian and Sicilian muses thought it cleverer to weave the one and the many together—by 'Ionian muses' he undoubtedly means Heraclitus. At this point, it is said of these Ionian muses who speak through Heraclitus, that they thought more sharply than the Sicilians in that they did not just teach about the alternation of multiplicity and unity, of global periods of dispersion and of coming back together into a unity, as Empedocles' didactic poem did. The sharper thesis is the simultaneity of the one and the many, the simultaneity of self-dispersing and self-unifying. What is ascribed to Heraclitus here is the idea that the one and the many are the whole truth of being, not alternatively, but in one. In reference to this, Plato has the stranger from Elea quote a statement from Heraclitus. This statement is encountered one more time in Plato where it is cited by the physician, Eryximachus (*Symposium* 187a). As with most Greek citations, the precise formulation of this statement is uncertain. It is, of course, a feature of the elegance of this kind of writing that wherever possible one does not use literal quotations, but rather one builds them into one's own thought processes—one of the main difficulties that the Greeks present for us is to divine where a quotation begins and to what extent there is an accommodation to their own way of thinking.[3] The statement legitimated by Plato reads: *diapheromenon aei sympheretai* (*Sophist* 242e). Corresponding to this is: *to hen gar phêsi diapheromenon auto hautôi sympheresthai hôsper harmonian toxou te kai lyras* (*Symposium* 187a; see Fragments 51 and 8). In English, this means: "The one that places itself apart from itself joins itself together with itself."

A most highly paradoxical formulation. Heraclitus loves to give examples of such paradoxes. Thus, in the *Symposium* he continues: "like the harmony of the bow and the lyre." And, somewhat similarly: "The barley drink that is not stirred separates itself."[4] Heraclitus illustrates his real wisdom, his *sophon*, in many such examples. In the *Symposium*, the same phrase that is encountered in the *Sophist* is placed in the mouth of the physician, Eryximachus, and this is significant. His inability to

---

3. The Stoics called this accommodation *ounoikeioun*.
4. Fragment 125: *kai ho kukeôn diístatai <'mê'> kinoumenos*.

understand the speculative unity of opposites is caricatured in the way the doctor exercises a high-handed critique of Heraclitus. The *Sophist* passage shows unequivocally that Plato understood very well that Heraclitus did not, like Eryximachus, intend the unity to emerge as the final result (*epeita hysteron homologêsantôn, Symposium* 187b 1). On the contrary: the main thing is precisely the simultaneity (see Fragment 18: *to antizoun sympheron*). Thus we have here a secure point of departure that is confirmed, moreover, by innumerable variations of the same thing. The question is how to bring together the Heracliteanism of existing things that are constantly in flux and the tense dialectical unity that is, as it were, squeezed together into such statements.

Let us proceed from the phenomena that Heraclitus has in mind. There is the river into which everything flows in constant change. But it is the same river.[5] In the end, the river, too, is an example of the unity of opposites of which Heraclitus speaks in countless phrases: war and peace, hunger and satiety, mortals and immortals, gods and men, and so on—a raft of extreme oppositions. He maintains that they are all one. The example of the river works best here in terms of the unity of the course of the river and the restlessness of its flow. The mysterious problem that shows itself behind all of these oppositions is apparently the fact that what is the same shows itself as an other *with no transition*. At issue in all of these examples is what the Greeks called 'metabolê,' abrupt change. It is distinguished by its precipitous suddenness. The fundamental experience of thinking here seems to be the essential unreliability of everything that shows itself sometimes in this way and sometimes in another. In the very next moment it can be different again and no longer present itself in this way. The insight into the unreliability of all things that already clearly underlies Eleatic thinking no doubt also inspired Plato's thinking of the *eidos*. As I see it, the ironic artificiality with which the Heracliteans in the *Theaetetus* are introduced speaks to the fact that Plato first erected the counter-construct to the universal flux in order to outline his thinking of the *eidos*. Perhaps he was also already encountering the doctrine

5. Plato, *Cratylus* 402a: *eiê ton auton...*; and with obvious reference to Heraclitus, Fragment 12: *potamoisi toisin autoisin embainousin hetera kai hetera hudata epirrei...*

itself in Cratylus and other 'genuine' Heracliteans. This seems to
me to follow indirectly from the way in which the Eleatic theme
is deferred in the *Theaetetus*. In a way that awakens a certain
tension, this part of the text prefigures more than just Eleatic
thinking and, in particular, the *Sophist*. I think the reason why
Socrates leaves the doctrine of Parmenides aside speaks even
more clearly here: "because, otherwise, that for the sake of
which we are engaged in our discussion, the essence of knowledge, would remain unexamined"[6]—as if knowledge would be at
all understandable without Eleatic thinking. Evidently, this is
indeed the precise doctrine that Theaetetus has to draw from
his conversation with Socrates, and it is for this reason that the
lead role in the conversation on the next day is transferred into
the hands of the stranger from Elea. In this discussion of the
Sophists, Theaetetus first learns what knowledge is: not immediate evidence, but *logos*. But, as to whether Heraclitus himself
would also have had to learn this first...? The process theory that
Socrates develops in the *Theaetetus* from the doctrine of flux
has its strongest support in Heraclitus' statement about the
always new waters that flow through the same rivers. This,
however, seems to point in a completely different direction:
"Souls, too, steam up from the moisture" (Fragment 12)—and it
is precisely their *logos* that seems unfathomable (Fragment 45).
This seems to be a profound suspicion of Heraclitus', and this is
precisely what the interests of modernity are particularly drawn
to. The structure of self-consciousness appears to be implicit
here—and the *logos* is, in fact, thought as the principle of the
world. Hegel *ante diem*.

   But how does this fit in with the rest of the tradition? Of
course, as everyone knows, this tradition bears the decisive
stamp of Aristotle. He is the main source for our knowledge of
the Presocratics in general. But, in Aristotle, matters involving
Heraclitus look quite bad. Aristotle tells us that some people
claim, evidently because of his paradoxical formulations,
that Heraclitus did not consider the basic principle of all knowledge, the principle of contradiction, to be valid (*Metaphysics*
Γ 3, 1005b 24). Even if he clearly did not take this polemical
assertion entirely seriously, in Aristotle's eyes, this could not be

---

   6. *Theaetetus* 184a 3 f.: *kai to megiston, hou heneka ho logos hôr-
mêtai, epistêmês peri ti not' estin, askepton genêtai.*

a recommendation. Of greater import is the fact that his real main concern, physics, can be connected to Heraclitus only with extraordinary difficulty. This leaves much to be considered. Aristotle's guiding perspective, which he sees confirmed in his scrutiny of the Presocratics and which he puts forward against Plato's Pythagoreanism, is not so much the articulation of a universe ordered in terms of numbers and proportions as it is the ontological constitution of 'nature' (*physis*) moving itself from out of itself: this intuition of the nature of the universe teaches us that it contains itself, it moves and orders itself, it is balanced within itself. Thus, in his eyes, Greek cosmology develops itself as the truth that lies at the heart of the cosmogonies of the most ancient thinkers, cosmogonies that were supported originally by religion and then more and more by scientific observation. The world needs no Atlas to carry it. It contains itself and holds itself in order. (This is also the case in the *Phaedo*, see 99b–c.)

What we know of Heraclitus does not fit this very well. The idea that what is is fundamentally fire is not very well suited to making the stable order of the universe or the story of its origination understandable. Obviously, the all-consuming fire cannot be prevented, by any limitations, from devouring everything. It does not allow itself to be properly compatible with the other 'elements.' With the help of arithmetic and the doctrine of proportions, Plato's *Timaeus* depicts for us how in the ordering of the universe it is not just earth and fire but (by means of air) water and fire, too, that are artfully held separate from one another (*Timaeus* 31b ff.). If Anaximander, one of the great Ionian inquirers prior to Heraclitus, is supposed to have explained the role of the heavenly bodies and their forms, he seems to have gotten himself into a serious predicament. The sun, the moon (provided that one does not know that it only has borrowed light), and the stars are certainly fire. But how can fire have such a clear form and outline and always illuminate in the same way? At this point, Anaximander comes upon the idea of the holes, the apertures in the great vault of the heavens through which the fire blazing behind it shines for us as an unperturbed illumination. Or so, at least, the doxography tells us (VS 12 A 11).

Now, there is certainly another way to think the mysterious essence of fire as a cosmic principle, and that is its presence in everything that is warm. The fact that the origin of life depends upon warmth has something illuminating about it, and we need only think of the doxography on Anaximander (12 A 30) in order to illustrate this. A material interpretation of fire as an element of things, however, is not provided here, and the testimonies for such an interpretation are not exactly promising. To be sure, in the *Cratylus* (413d 3), Plato mentions an interpretation of fire as 'the warm itself' (*auto to thermon*), which is within fire, but he does so in a context that is not only extremely playful but is also completely unsuited to a cosmogonical perspective. The *Cratylus* (413b 4, c 1) alludes much more to Heraclitus' idea of the sun that constantly rekindles itself (*neos eph hêmerê*, Fragment 6) or of the sun that never sets (*to mê dunon pote*, Fragment 16). Even the reference to Heraclitus' sun in the *Politeia* (*Republic* VI, 498a) testifies to the fact that this doctrine of Heraclitus' was quite well known, though it was certainly not famous for its cosmological progressiveness. In any case, nothing is reminiscent of Heraclitus in other passages in Plato where fire and heat appear as almost the same thing.[7] Aristotle barely mentions Heraclitus in his introductions to the *Physics* and the *Metaphysics*. Simplicius (in *Physics* 21, 1 ff.) puts forward a pure construct, stemming ostensibly from Theophrastus, and has quite a good look into its difficulties himself.[8]

Even if we assume fire to be in everything that is warm and therefore in everything that is alive, as we perhaps might on the basis of Plato,[9] the cosmological problem of fire remains difficult. It will not allow itself to be understood properly as an element, as a constituent. Aristotle does not know where to begin with this. Indeed, it is not easy to see how one would build a cosmology on the basis of the primal phenomenon of fire. Did Heraclitus construct a cosmology at all?

We have reasons to doubt this. In the first place, there is an ancient tradition that, in my view, we have not taken seriously enough. Apparently, the impression made by Aristotle and Theophrastus is so strong that we view all of the Presocratics the same way, as cosmologists. In Ciceronian times, Diodotus, a

7. E.g., *Phaedo* 103d f.; *Philebus* 29b f.
8. He says (in *Physics* 203, 24–25 in Diels): *kai dechesthai ta enantia pur menon ou pephuke. toutou de aition to drastikon einai mallon auto kai eidei analogein, all' ouchi hylê*. Neither the Aristotelian concept of *hylê* nor the Empedoclean concept of the elements is appropriate for 'that which is active' (*to drastikon*).
9. E.g., *Philebus* 29c or *Timaeus* 79d.

Stoic who still knew the Heraclitus text, passed down to us the idea that the text of Heraclitus did not deal with nature at all but rather with the 'politeia,' the state. Whatever was said in it about nature would only have been said for purposes of illustration.[10]—Yet we must ask ourselves whether this was really just a moralistic Stoic reinterpretation, as the reputed title undoubtedly suggests ("A Precise Compass for the Direction of Life"[11]), or whether there is something true in it. In any case, when we scrutinize the mass of Heraclitus citations we find a very large number of evidently political and moralistic statements that exert a powerful appeal. Again and again, for example, there is a bitter critique of the political blindness and imprudence of his fellow countrymen. We also have other passages, all of which belong to the moral/political dimension. Semantic evidence points in this same direction. In Greek usage, the word 'phronêsis' is, for the most part, 'practical reasonableness' and thus does not connote so much the theoretical use of reason.[12] Thus there is an entire list of indications advising us to take the cited utterances of the Stoic seriously.[13] We must ask ourselves whether Heraclitus was a rival of the Ionian cosmologists at all and not more likely one of their critics—just as Parmenides no doubt also functioned as such a critic.

How are we supposed to decide such a question when the tradition does not just leave us in the lurch but leads us into error with even greater zeal? It is not just the interests of the meta-physician, Aristotle, that steer us in this direction. The moralistic over-interpretation of this supposed cosmology by the later Stoics and Church Fathers imports something foreign into it as well, the world conflagration. For the Church Fathers

10. VS 22 A 1 (DK I 142, 31): ... *(hos) ou (phêsi) peri phuseôs einai to suggramma, alla peri politeias, ta de peri phuseôs en paradeigmatos eidei keisthai.*

11. VS 22 A 1 (DK I 142, 18): *akribes oiakisma pros otathmen biou.*

12. Thus Werner Jaeger (*Die Theologie der frühen griechischen Denker*, Stuttgart 1953, p. 121 ff., and the annotations therein) has convincingly called attention to the fact that, in distinction to Parmenides, the Greek words that Heraclitus used for 'thinking' are not *noein* and *nous* but rather *phronein* and *phronêsis.*

13. Meanwhile, as I mention, Kahn does this (p. 21). I agree with him completely that this does not mean that Heraclitus would be conceivable without Ionian cosmology. It is present and remains in view, but in such a way that the critique of the *polymathiê* is directed at it.

this was, conceptually speaking, the fire of Hell. They could presuppose that Heraclitus already knew something of this. This is how they understood his doctrine of fire. They were also familiar with the fact that the Stoics had taught the doctrine of the world conflagration, the 'ekpurôsis.' In Christian theology, the conflagration of the world becomes the judgment of the world. But does the Heraclitean statement that all of this seems to go back to really say that everything goes up in flames? It is Fragment 66: *panta gar, phêsi, to pur epelthon krinei kai katalêpsetai.*

What is the proper translation? As a rule, we understand the pair of Greek verbs as 'to condemn' and as 'to grasp' or, perhaps, 'take into custody.' Indeed these are words that are familiar to us as legal expressions and, to that extent, fit the idea of the Last Judgment. Hippolytus then, with great enthusiasm, also quotes the statement in this way. But *krinein* primarily means 'to cut, to differentiate, to separate.' The statement can thus very well mean that fire separates everything.[14] Everything is burned in the incandescence of fire until it disintegrates into ashes. This is precisely why *katalambanein* is far from always meaning 'to take into custody,' but its primary meaning is instead simply 'to grasp, to lay hold of.' This is, indeed, the fire that can bring everything into its glow so that even the stones (coals) become fiery as they glow in the flames—a beautiful, intuitive example of the fact that even the earth 'becomes fire.'[15] The magma of the volcano is a good illustration of this. Thus the statement invoked for *ekpurôsis* in Heraclitus could have had a completely different meaning than the one that, as a rule, has been imposed upon it. But, who knows? Nevertheless, we must consider the fact that the statement *primarily* has the sense exhibited here—and, at most, the underlying 'moral' sense should be allowed to resonate. This, of course, is only a hypothesis that cannot act as a self-sufficient authority. Nevertheless, there

14. This is what it means in Empedocles (VS 31 B 62): *krineinomenon pur.* If this is supposed to be an unusual use of *krinein,* it is a Heraclitus citation!

15. At this point, Bywater cites the passage 'Aetna,' V. 536: *quod si quis lapidis miratur fusile robur, cogitet obscuri verissima dicta libelli, Heracliti, tui, nihil insuperabile ab igni, omnia quo rerum naturae semina iacta.*

are still some supporting indicators for this statement and its interpretation, and we find them, above all, in the etymological play of the *Cratylus* (412f.). There fire is mentioned, as 'the warm itself' that is within fire (413c 3), along with *helios* and Anaxagorean *nous*, as something that permeates all appearances and is brought into connection with what is just (the *dikaion*). This is indeed 'Heraclitean' in the sense of the *Cratylus* to the extent that, in its relative quickness, this fastest and smallest (*tachiston kai leptotaton* 412d 5) lets everything else appear as what is (*hôste chrêsthai hôsper hestôsi tois allois* 412d 7)—in exactly the same way that the theory of motion in the *Theaetetus* (156c ff.) interprets 'being.' In any case, this *Cratylus* witticism best reflects how the just, the *dikaion*, is filled up, as it were, with materiality by means of the fire that penetrates everything.[16]

Let us ask ourselves how we are able to proceed any further at all in the uncertainty that comes over us in this situation that we have inherited. In my opinion, there is only one methodological point of entry: the *morphological* one. We can work out the structure of the unambiguous statements that can only belong to Heraclitus because they are all as similar to each other as family members. This is not to claim that we could differentiate the imitations or the reinterpretations from the genuine Heraclitus sayings with certainty in each individual case. Even family resemblance, of course, has no original image against which similarities can be measured (Wittgenstein's metaphor made this suitable for the critique of nominalistic prejudices). Thus the fact that it furnishes no strict criteria in no way speaks against the guiding idea of a morphological investigation. Moreover, even where imitations are present, the thought structure that is being imitated may not be entirely unrecognizable; and, if this is so, the imitation presents some guidance. For example, following the path of morphologically guided reduction, I have reclaimed a fragment that was heretofore missing from the collections, even though in the most reliable place—the list of Hippolytus citations—it is transmitted to us as expressly Heraclitean.[17] However, as it occurs in Hippolytus, it is so alienating to what is Christian/Trinitarian that one takes it to be a sheer

---

16. See *Cratylus* 412d ff. and 413b ff. (*boulomenoi apopimplanai me*) the sequence: *hêlios—pur—thermon—nous*.
17. See "On the Tradition of Heraclitus," in this volume, page 27 ff.

fabrication. It can be reconstructed in a morphological way. The outcome reads as follows: "The father is the son of himself." This wants to read: When the father produces a son, he turns himself into a father. This seems to me to be a genuinely Heraclitean statement in the terse style of a paradox, which is why the later style critics said that he had been a melancholic and that he only ever uttered his statements in halves. This is nevertheless a directive for us, a reasonable guiding principle: Wherever something appears terse, concentrated, paradoxical, there we have Heraclitus.

It fits in with this guiding principle that one of the artistic modes that plays a predominating role in Heraclitus corresponds nicely to such a paradoxical style: the pun. A pun is based on the sudden shift from one already accomplished orientation of meaning and understanding into a completely different one. There is a famous example of this in Heraclitus: "The name of the bow is life, its deed is death."[18] This depends on the consonance of the word 'bios' for both life and bow. Within the word, there is already a unity of opposites. This is surely the reason why Heraclitus especially loves puns. They permit him to capture his own truth in the wording and to stir up, as it were, our flattened out, thoughtless familiarity with language. Another example that plays with words in this way in order to reinforce the truth that is veiled within them is Fragment 114, where the consonance between 'common' (*xunon*) and 'with reason' (*xun nôi*) constitutes the pun,[19] and something is expressed in this pun. Not only is reason common to all things, but everything that is common is based on reason. Anything else may be unknowable for us. Based on the citations in Aristotle[20] and the plays on *eros* by Pausanias and Eryximachus in the *Symposium*—and based on the background of the Hesiodic model (*Works and Days*, 20 ff.)—I suspect that Heraclitus plays with *eros* and *eris* in a similar way—in view of the 'loving strife' to which, it seems to me, Aristotle is alluding.[21]

18. Fragment 48: *tôi oun toxôi onoma bios, ergon de thanatos.*
19. Fragment 114: *xun nôi legontas ischyrizesthai chrê tôi xunôi pantôn, hokôsper nomôi polis, kai polu ischyroterôs...*
20. *Nicomachean Ethics* Θ 1, 1155b 4; *Eudemian Ethics* H 1, 1235a 25.
21. *Nicomachean Ethics* Θ 1, 1155b 6: *panta kat' erin ginesthai.* Compare this to Heraclitus, Fragment 80: *...kai ginomena panta kat' erin kai chreôn.*

The fact that other artistic modes point in this same direction, modes such as the paradoxical sentence, the parable, the parallelism, and the asymmetrical analogy, has been shown by many scholars and by Hermann Fraenkel in particular. It is therefore valid to unlock the paradoxical insights of Heraclitus by proceeding from the morphological.

I shall begin with a well known statement that gives me the opportunity to display the awkwardness of the preconceptions implicit in the way these passages are cited. The statement is handed down to us in Plotinus (among others), and this fact is, in turn, of value for our interpretation. This Platonist from the time of the Caesars is one for whom new dimensions of interiority had already opened up. Thus it is self-evident for us that his understanding of the Heraclitean book (which he still knew) struck out in directions altogether different from those we can assume for Heraclitus himself and, yet again, altogether different from those of textbooks rooted ultimately in the Aristotelian/ Theophrastian tradition and their readers. The statement I am referring to is one of the simplest statements that one can think of: "The way up and down is one and the same" (or: "The way there and back is one and the same").[22] In antiquity, people frequently already understood this from the perspective of Aristotelian influenced cosmology, and they saw in it a depiction of the cycle of the elements as it describes the great rotation of elements from below to above, from above to below, from the heavenly fire to water and to air, if not the reverse, and from there to earth.[23] Yet, neither in Plotinus nor elsewhere does the text point in any way to this context. Only later reappropriations interpret it cosmologically. In Plotinus, it is his fundamental predisposition toward transcendence, the predisposition of the early Christian centuries, that thoroughly determines the horizon of the author's understanding. This is why he understands the statement to be about the soul that descends into the body and about its return, its ascent toward the one and the true. For Plotinus, this is the way up and the way down that Heraclitus is supposed to have intended. Certainly no one today would follow this interpretation of Heraclitus' proposition. We become

22. Fragment 60: *hodos anô katô mia kai hôutê*.
23. See Bywater, p. 28. Clement also understood Fragment 31 in this way.

completely sure of this when we read in Plotinus how he praises
Heraclitus in particular because Heraclitus has taught us to
search for our souls, our true selves.

Nevertheless, for us, the Heraclitus statements to which
Plotinus assigns this orientation still have something seductive
about them. Here we read, for example: "I have sought myself."[24] For ancient biographical science, this meant that he had
no teacher but found out everything for himself instead. For
us, this resonates like an early intimation of Christian interiority,
as it is to be heard for the first time in Socratic questioning—especially when we read: "The limits of the soul cannot be surveyed,
however broadly one strides, so deeply lies its ground."[25] Again,
this resonates with Socrates and Plato, those 'anima naturaliter
christiana' who, in the very heart of the Silenian shrine, recognized what is truly beautiful and generally pointed the way the
Christian future.[26] And yet here, too, we should be mistrustful of
the overtones of our own account of the soul. In any case, whatever our statement ("The way up and the way down is one and
the same") may be about, it is thus surely more correct to recognize in it an utterly straightforward observation. It is the same
path that seems so difficult in the ascent and so easy in the
descent (or, the same path that seems so long on the way there
seems so short on the return trip). I think it is a straightforward
example of how one and the same thing can look quite different,
even opposed.

An entire genre of statements has been handed down under
the name of Heraclitus that announce in a similar way how
something can change its aspect completely. Evidently the structure of the ideas corresponds to the formal structure of such
statements. What Heraclitus wants to say is clear: that, contrary to our own experience of distinguishing one thing from
another, of opposing one to the other, we should realize that
whatever might present itself so differently also harbors a kind of
identity within the opposition itself. Heraclitus sees through the

24. Fragment 101: *edizêsamên emeôuton.*
25. Fragment 45: *Psychês peirata iôn ouk an exeuroio, pasan epi-
poreuomenos hodon: houtô bathyn logon echei.*
26. *Symposium*, 221d–222a: Alcibiades likens Socrates to a statue
of Silenus which must be opened, and in the center of which one finds
images of the gods.

apparentness of the different and the opposite and everywhere discovers the one. This need not preclude the idea that still other, morally emphatic, applications are meant to resonate in the statement about the path, applications that were precisely what was really intended. His *logos*, however, is the one. He discerns this in such diverse phenomena as the flow of things, the abrupt change from fire into water and from sleep to waking, and he discovers the same riddle in everything—in the flame that consumes itself and is extinguished, in the motion that begins by itself and ceases by itself. Everywhere he sees the wonder of life, the riddle of being conscious (being awake), and the mystery of death.

This will show itself to be one of the points at which Plato positively appropriates the heritage of Heraclitean thinking. In any case, Plotinus' use of citations teaches us how little obligation we have to apply the statement cosmologically. On the contrary, our right to a simple understanding of the statement surely can be justified by looking to Heraclitus himself and especially the beginning of his text.[27] By a fortunate accident, it has been handed down to us in good shape. Aristotle, referring to the first statement of Heraclitus' text, remarks that what we have before us is a punctuation problem: "This *logos* that always is, about which human beings always remain without understanding...."[28] Aristotle asks himself where the 'always' belongs. Even modern philologists are divided about this. Is it the *logos* that always is, or does the *logos* always remain without understanding? Presumably, this is an actual case of what grammarians call *apo koinou*. By itself an utterly pedantic excuse of the school master, this category comes to life in listening to such a statement. We must recall that Aristotle was, first and foremost, a reader (albeit, of course, one who read aloud). This text, however, was surely intended to be a lecture. The speaker could thus articulate it in such a way that the word 'always' could shed light on both sides and color the surrounding words.[29] Yet, at this point, I am going into this much discussed statement,

27. See my study, "Hegel und Heraklit", in GW 7: *Plato im Dialog* (Tübingen: J. C. B. Mohr, 1991), 32–42. [The abbreviation GW refers throughout to Gadamer's ten-volume *Gesammelte Werke*.]

28. Fragment 1: *tou de logou toud' eontos aei axunetoi gigontai anthrôpoi....*

29. It does not seem possible to me, as has been verified many times, to relate the 'always' exclusively to the *logos*, in the sense of 'the *logos* that

a statement that outdoes itself in paradoxes, in order to emphasize one paradox that seems to me not to have been properly considered until now and which supposedly presents a kind of
guideline for a collective interpretation. Heraclitus describes his
intentions here in the following way: *kata physin diaireôn hekaston kai phrazôn hokôs echei.* This sounds highly conventional,
like an declaration in the style of a comprehensive *historiê.*
Heraclitus promises "to explain everything like it really is." But
what does this explanation really look like? The reader of the
book sees it, the listener to the *logos* hears it. The Heraclitean
message is not differentiation, exactly, but perceiving the one
in everything that is differentiated. What others take to be different, as Hesiod takes day and night, is in fact and in truth
one and the same. The Heraclitean doctrine is constantly formulated in this way: *hen to sophon.*[30] I consider this to be the
authentic and original principle that Heraclitus appears to be
repeating many times in his book. The principle can extend in
different directions according to the formulation, *hen to sophon*:
"it does and does not want to be called by the name of Zeus"
(Fragment 32), or, "this is insight" (*gnôme*, Fragment 41).
Our formulation, 'the wise is one,' is also hiding somehow in
Fragment 50.[31]

What appears here as 'the wise' is an extremely polyphonic
neuter. The Greek's possession of the neuter constitutes one of

is true' (*eôn logos*). Such a possibility is ruled out if one considers the
position of this *ontos* after the unitary/monolithic *logou.* Aristotle does well
to leave things undecided where no decision is necessary. The fact that
he is aware of it as a problem at all seems to illustrate for us a transition
toward a primary mode of reading that is interested in punctuation as an
aid to understanding. However, the truth is that the punctuation is actually
less important than the resonant tone that can be understood in a throughly
ambivalent way in this psalming lecture. Similar to Kahn, p. 93 f., except
that I do not understand the *ontos aei* as 'forever true,' but rather as 'ever
present' (and thereby 'true')—'present' and yet 'ignored.' What Kahn has
shown us in his groundbreaking study of the meanings of 'being' is valid not
just for Heraclitus, but also for the idea that *nothing here* can be separate:
'present' and 'true,' said from out of the *logos* are one, even if it always (*aei*)
remains misunderstood.

30. See Fragment 41: *einai gar hen to sophon, epistasthai gnomên,
hoteêi kubernaitai panta dia pantôn*; Fragment 32: *hen to sophon mounon
legesthai ouk ethelei kai ethelei Zênos onoma.*

31. Fragment 50: *ouk emou, alla tou logou akousantas homologein
sophon estin hen panta einai.*

their ingenious advantages for abstraction in thinking. Reinhardt and Snell have taught us to see this. We are acquainted with a similar use of the neuter from German poetry, primarily since Goethe and Hölderlin, who use 'das Göttliche' (the divine) or 'das Rettende' (that which saves or redeems) in their poems. When things like this are encountered in a poem, they are not to be understood as definite entities.[32] Rather, a presence of being emanates from such a neuter, a presence that fills the entire space. 'Das Unheimliche' (the uncanny), like 'das Rettende,' 'das Göttliche,' or 'das Heilige' (the holy), or whatever it is, is the fullest presence, without the idea that a determinate entity would be named by it. So, too, 'das Weise' (that which is wise) is not one kind of thing among many others—it is 'separated' from everything (*pantôn kechôrismenon*, Fragment 108). As opposed to the appearance of changing differences, it is that which really is. This is how Heraclitus evidently intended his *logos*, a truth that speaks from out of everything and yet a truth that no one wishes to acknowledge as the truth.

To me, in any case, the hermeneutic task in understanding this introductory statement seems to be not to interpret it in advance by approaching it from out of a later doctrine. A declaration, instead, is supposed to awaken the expectation of and base itself on the style of *historiê*—yet this declaration constantly disrupts this expectation in the most highly paradoxical way.[33] The proem, after all, does not declare that the author has a doctrine that is better than the doctrines of others. Heraclitus is far more ambitious. It is supposed to be better than all of the points of view that other human beings in general

32. See "Sokrates' Frömmigkeit des Nichtwissens", GW, Bd. 7, p. 85 ff.
33. A. P. Mourelatos ("Heraclitus, Parmenides, and the Naive Metaphysics of Things," in *Exegesis and Argument: Studies in Greek Philosophy Presented to Gregory Vlastos*, eds. E. N. Lee, A. P. D. Mourelatos, and R. M. Rorty, Assen: Van Gorcum, 1973, p. 38, note 60.) would like to avoid the triviality in this text by understanding the *hopôs echei* as the pregnant 'holding together' that is actually the wisdom of Heraclitus. In my view, the fact that we are dealing here with the first statement of the book speaks against this. This declaration is not yet the doctrine. On the contrary, as the declaration of something that, in truth, attains its fulfillment in an entirely different sense, the conventionality of these statements appears to me to be highly paradoxical. I will attempt to demonstrate this.

have. Heraclitus is as radical as Parmenides is when the goddess Parmenides introduces speaks of the opinions of mortals
(Fragments 1, 30, and 6). The fact that this is not a reference
to Parmenides' colleagues should finally be accepted. Unfor-
tunately, it is not so rigorously observed that these 'viewpoints'
(*doxai*) of the mortals always appear in the plural and not at all
in the Platonic singular.[34]

I maintain that the proem tells us nothing of the content of
the doctrine. Nevertheless, right at its beginning there is a genuine
Heraclitean simile that presents a first hint of what Heraclitus
wants to say on the whole. Here, too, the theme is still the opposition between the one knower and the many who do not know:
"What human beings do while awake remains concealed from
them, just as they forget what they do while asleep."[35] Evidently,
this means that they learn nothing from the wealth of their
experiences.[36] This is what distinguishes our activities in sleep.
When we are awake, we forget them. From the dream experiences that we have undergone we take nothing over into
our lived reality. The activities in dreams are inconsequential.
Awakened to the wakefulness of the day, neither are we able
to continue playing the game of the dream, nor does it inter-
polate itself into our experience. This is what the introductory
statement wants to tell us. Therefore, it is not a question of the
extent to which in ancient life dreams would have been understood in terms of their augury. Heraclitus looks with cold and
clear eyes at the fact that dreaming is precisely not being awake.

34. See my study of this Parmenides passage in GW, Bd. 7, p. 24 ff.
35. Fragment 1: *tous... anthrôpous lanthanei hokosa egerthentes
poiousin hokôsper hokosa heudontes epilanthanontai.*
36. Karl Reinhardt (*Kosmos und Sympathie*, Munich 1926, p. 195),
adopting Hölscher's understanding of the last statement (Uvo Hölscher,
Anfängliches Fragen. Studien zur frühen griechischen Philosophie, Göttingen
1968, p. 157), cannot convince me. One expects the preceding *apeiroisin/
peirômenoi* to be illustrated here. (Just as in Kahn, p. 99.) The statement
is pointedly symmetrical. The subtlety of the parallel between *lanthanei* and
epilanthanontai lies in its variation: despite their being awake, human
beings live in permanent forgetfulness (*lanthanei*), just as they forget after-
wards (*epi*) their dreams (what they did while asleep) and leave them
unheeded (*epilanthanontai*). We encounter the same variation in the parallels in Fragment 21 where we expect *enypnion* and find *hypnos*, an
entire period of time. I also cannot follow Bollack here because he neglects
the clear evidence that it is the forgetting of dreams that is being alluded to.

The idea that human beings undergo experiences without becoming wise means that they live like dreamers. Their experiences have no consequences. And so it literally says: *apeiroisin eoikasin peirômenoi*, "they are the same as the inexperienced despite all of their experience."

In this way, the beginning of the book provides a guideline, not just for grasping the compression of the Heraclitean style, but also for seeking that which is one, the 'wise,' behind the most ordinary experience.

The metaphor in this vehement introductory statement is rather suspenseful. The incomprehension that human beings have regarding the truth is not to be posited simply as an immutable fact. One can awaken someone from sleep. The emphatic impact of the first statement depends upon this. But it is more than this; it is, at the same time, an assertion that turns back upon itself, so to speak. What announces itself here as the doctrine of Heraclitus is a true paradox. This doctrine travels the path toward insight and, at the same time, teaches us about the gulf that stands between the one truth and our inability to learn due to our entanglement in the manifold of human illusions and dreams. The simile of waking and sleeping is not just an emphatic appeal, it belongs at the same time to the content of Heraclitus' doctrine.

We thus encounter it repeatedly (even if perhaps not always in Heraclitean wording, as when the word 'kosmos' is used for 'world'). For Heraclitus, the dream is a symbol for general incomprehension. A case in point is a statement like, "For those who are awake there is one and only one common world, while those who sleep each turn away into their own."[37] In this sense, because of their dreaming, Fragment 75 calls the one who is asleep, *ergatas* (worker: builder of a world all his own).[38] His gaze is always turned toward the people who, in waking, behave like ones who are asleep. Fragment 73 speaks to this directly:

37. Fragment 89: *tois egrêgorosin hena kai koinon kosmon einai, tôn de koimômenôn hekaston eis idion apostrephesthai.*
38. Fragment 75: *tous katheudontas... ergatas einai... kai synergous tôn en tôi kosmôi ginomenôn.* In my opinion, Walter Bröcker (*Die Geschichte der Philosophie vor Sokrates*, Frankfurt am Main: Vittorio Klostermann, 1965, p. 35 ff.) rightly separates the Stoic addition here, *kai synergous*, from the Heraclitean statement cited by Marcus Aurelius.

"One should not act and speak like those who are asleep."[39] Admittedly, this formulation is so banal that we might well have to assume, along with Kirk,[40] that here Marcus Aurelius is simply articulating the moral gist of the concluding sentence of Fragment 1.

We repeatedly encounter a parallelism formed between waking and sleeping, on one hand, and living and being dead on the other. The fact that comparisons, analogies, and parallelisms constituted an archaic mode of thinking has been demonstrate primarily by Hermann Fraenkel.[41] Nevertheless, the Heraclitean use of this mode of thinking has its own character. We can observe how Heraclitus does not simply construct such parallelisms and comparisons; rather, he loves to elaborate on them in a paradoxical way so that they attain a provocative/paranetic sharpness. Thus, we do not read in Fragment 21, as we might expect, a correspondence between sleep and the apparitions of dreams, on the one hand, and being awake and the waking world (life), on the other. Instead, surprisingly and provocatively, it reads: "Death [not life] is what we see awake; what we see as slumberers, sleep."[42] The subtlety of this surprising parallel lies in the fact that the concluding term reads *hypnos* and not *enypnion*, 'sleep' and not 'dream.' The one who is sleeping thereby construes the overall condition of sleep, encountered in the apparitions of dreaming, as that which he sees. In this way, the precision of this finely wrought statement clearly emerges. The two standard tropes are formed by death and sleep, the correspondence of which speaks for itself. What is provocative about the comparison lies in the fact that it begins surprisingly. In the first clause, 'life' would fit the progress of the statement, and there it reads 'death.' Thus, as a whole, what is seen in being awake, along with its apparent wakefulness, is itself ascribed not to being alive but rather to being dead.[43]

39. Fragment 73: *ou dei hôsper katheudontas poiein kai legein…*

40. G. S. Kirk, *Heraclitus: The Cosmic Fragments*, Cambridge 1954, p. 44 ff.

41. H. Fraenkel, *Wege und Formen, Frühgriechisches Denken* (Munich: Beck, 1955), p. 258 ff.

42. Fragment 21: *Thanatos estin hokosa egerthentes horeomen, hokosa de heudontes hypnos.*

43. Kahn, p. 213, does indeed detect the asymmetry of the Heraclitean sentence, but in my opinion he seeks it in the wrong place.

The family resemblances among Heraclitean statements requires a very careful rhythmic analysis of their tradition. In the meantime, I find very fine observations in Charles Kahn's commentary. In that I am looking in the same direction, sometimes I would like to go even further and, through emendation and condensation, reproduce the original Heraclitean statement from statements that are not quite so well forged. In precisely the most well forged of Heraclitus' statements I think I recognize a true family resemblance. Thus, with regard to Kahn's analysis of the phonic structure of Fragment 25,[44] I would like to pose the question of whether, at the end, *lagchanousi* ('they receive') is not superfluous. The word is perhaps due to the ancient technique of citing and explicating simultaneously. The statement could simply have read: *moroi mezones mezones moirai* (or, *mezonas moiras*). The clear word play speaks for itself and demands consideration.

Conversely, we feel sure of having the correct wording when a statement displays clear standard tropes, as does Fragment 21 in the correspondence between *thanatos* and *hypnos* ('death' and 'sleep'). Fragment 20[45] also exhibits such tropes with *genomenoi* and *genesthai*. In this last case I ask myself whether the connection of the standard tropes in such a long statement would not be more effective if we were to go still further and bring *morous t' echein* face to face with *morous genesthai*. It is certainly clear that *ethelousi* should not be separated completely from its object, *zôein*; indeed, this is reinforced by the *te—kai*. But why should Heraclitus have followed the double-turning gravitation of words only in his introductory statement and not have exploited their bivalence elsewhere as well? Here, just as 'always' does in Fragment 1, *ethelousi* would double itself in hearing it: *genomenoi zôein ethelousi morous te echein kai [paidas kataleipousi] morous genesthai*. I think I recognize this as a stylistic element in which *echein* and *genesthai* confront each other.[46]

In the same way, the fragment that I have reconstructed, *patêr huios heautou*, seems convincing to me (and to a few

44. Kahn, p. 231 ff.

45. Fragment 20: *genomenoi zôein ethelousi morous t' echein, mallon de anathauesthai, kai paidas kataleipousi morous genesthai*.

46. With regard to the effacement of *mallon anapauesthai*, see Karl Reinhardt in *Hermes* 1942, p. 4.

others). In Fragment 21, dream and sleep stand for the delusion that consists in the fact that we are not in a position to recognize one and the same essence in all the various things that we encounter. In innumerable variations, Heraclitus never tires of teaching the inseparability of opposites that signifies their unity. The above-mentioned introductory statement also belongs among these. Indeed, when a multiplicity is declared in it—the 'words and deeds' as everyone encounters them—we must simultaneously keep in mind precisely the one that alone is the true. The statement shows all humanity falling into the same error of taking what is opposed as separate entities instead of recognizing their true unity. This is the paradox—that he wants to 'lay out' or 'unfold' this one/being; and this is the *logos* to which it is proper to listen. He does not just mean what everyone knows, the 'one-after-another,' the necessary dissolution of one thing by another, like day and night, summer and winter, youth and old age; but rather, above and beyond this, he means the 'in-one-another' that Plato emphasizes in the passage from the *Sophist* with which we began. Evidently, the tension of these Ionian muses consists in the fact that it is the same thing that holds itself together in its separation from itself (Fragment 51), like the mixed drink that would separate if one did not stir it (Fragment 125), or like Fragment 10 with its *sunaidon/diaidon* ('consonant/dissonant'), or Fragment 8 with its *antixoun/sympheron* ('striving against/helping with'). In Aristotle, it becomes completely clear how this is to be understood: the high and the low note must both be there if there is to be harmony.[47] The stepping apart into opposites, therefore, is not the result of a process of *ekkrisis*, as Aristotle maintains with regard to Anaximander (VS 12 A16) and as perhaps is actually the case behind the profound doctrine of opposites that Parmenides' goddess unveils to him. Nowhere, in fact, does Aristotle have a speculative understanding of Heraclitus' contradictory assertions.[48] In a passage in the *Physics* (A4, 187a 20 ff.), it becomes

47. *Eudemian Ethics*, H 1, 1235a 25; *Nicomachean Ethics*, Θ 1, 1155b 4.
48. This is shown clearly at *Metaphysics*, Γ 3, 1005b 23 ff.: *adunaton gar hontinoun tauton hypolambanein einai kai mê einai, kathaper tines oiontai legein Herakleiton.* Likewise at Γ 7,1012a 24 ff.: *eoike d' ho men Herakleitou logos, legôn panta einai kai mê einai, hapanta alêthê poiein.*

immediately apparent—through a similar differentiation between 'periodically' and 'uniquely,' in fact—that, aside from Anaximander, he mentions only Empedocles and Anaxagoras as being among those who adopt the one and the many at the same time. Here, *ekkrisis* is spoken of, but apparently without Heraclitus being mentioned along with it; although that could have been expected given Aristotle's reliance on the *Sophist* passage at 242b. Likewise, Heraclitus is not named in the *Metaphysics* (A8, 989a 13) when Aristotle substitutes the mediator between fire and air, which he speaks of in the *Physics* (187a 14) with what mediates between air and water. At this point, instead of classifying Heraclitus' doctrine of fire as a case of *ekkrisis* and fitting it into the principle of his own doctrine of elements, Aristotle overlooks him. In Aristotle's eyes, apparently, this was not reconcilable with the Heraclitean text.

So, in any case, we must judge whether to take the Platonic idea of cashing in on the Heraclitean Ionian muses as opposed to the Sicilian muses of Empedocles at face value. There is, however, a series of undoubtedly Heraclitean statements that support this: the image of the river, the harmony in the connection between bow and lyre, harmony as such, the barley drink. In all of these cases, the discussion is no longer of a unity based on sheer temporal succession or on the sheer suddenness of transition. (In any event, if what we had in mind were the suddenness of transition, we could subsume these examples under a rubric that excludes the simultaneity of the speculative unity of temporal succession.)

How do the stronger conceptual assertions look now? Fragment 10[49] certainly leads in the direction of a prior separation, and yet, since the Platonic *sympheromenon/diapheromenon* crops up in the list, it also clearly intends simultaneity. This is precisely why we can only understand the *hola kai ouch hola* as the logical inseparability of the whole and parts; and, indeed, this is just how it is with the consonance and dissonance that are secured through the analogy of harmony (*synaidon/diaidon*). This once again establishes the meaning of 'the one from everything' in the sense in which Plato speaks of it.

---

49. Fragment 10 (= Pseudo-Aristotle, *De Mundo*, 5, 396b 20 f.): *synapsies* (or *sullapsies*) *hola kai ouch hola, sympheromenon diapheromenon, synaidon diaidon: kai ek pantôn hen kai ex henos panta.*

If we examine the prospectus for the citation list in Hippolytus (Fragment 51[50]), then for some of them, presumably, we can vacillate as to whether they illustrate genuine speculative unity. Nevertheless, my aforementioned analysis of the father-son paradox has fortified the expressive value of this citation list, and thus, generally speaking, wherever Hippolytus expressly brings forward genuine opposites, as in Fragment 67,[51] we must take the one in its Platonic sense. In the case of day and night, the Hesiod polemic in Fragment 57 confirms this. Likewise, death (*thanatos*) and its opposition to life is assured by Fragment 76, which goes back to Fragment 62.[52] Other assertions, however, seem to express only change as such and not the speculative unity that lies within change. This is perhaps valid for the concluding passage of Fragment 67,[53] where the various aspects of the god or of fire are realized through the admixture of various kinds of incense. Nevertheless, at this point 'the god' stands for the one as well. Fragment 88,[54] the reading of which is rather uncertain, no doubt lays the emphasis on change, on a succession that is nevertheless described as an abrupt shift (*metapesonta*). Just so, in Heraclitus' eyes every change implies a simultaneity. To me, this seems to be valid for the cosmology of Fragment 31, which we will discuss later.

This stepping apart into opposites, therefore, generally provides evidence of the unitary essence of things and their true being. Opposites do not exist without one another, whether it is the case that they necessarily succeed one another or whether they harmonize directly and form the unity of a melodic arrangement. In any case, we must come to the insight that the other is

---

50. Fragment 51: *ou xyniasin hokôs diapheromenon heôutôi sympheretai: palintonos harmoniê hokôsper toxou kai lyrês.*

51. Fragment 67: *ho theos hêmerê euphronê, cheimôn theros, polemos eirênê, koros limos....* "The god is day and night, winter and summer, war and peace, satiation and hunger."

52. Fragment 62: *athanatoi thnêtoi, thnêtoi athanatoi, zôntes ton ekeinôn thanaton, ton de ekeinôn bion tethneôtes.* For an interpretation, see the discussion below.

53. Fragment 67 (cont'd.): *...alloioutai de hokôsper pyr, hopotan symmigêi thuômasin, onomazetai kath' hêdonên hekastou.*

54. Fragment 88: *tauto t' eni zôn kai tethnêkos kai egrêgoros kai katheudon kai neon kai gêraion: tade gar metapesonta ekeina esti kakeina palin metapesonta tauta.*

always already there with it. The best indication of this is precisely that whatever is opposed bursts forth suddenly and immediately. All at once, that which is changes its appearance utterly,
and its opposite emerges. This proves that it was already there
beforehand. This is why I think that, fundamentally, Heraclitus
wants to maintain the same thing for everything—the being one
of what is different; and this is why he refers to the one as being
'separated from everything.' He clearly chooses to see those
opposites that he names explicitly from the point of view that,
though they are apparently excluded from one another altogether, they nevertheless allow themselves to be recognized as one
and the same thing.

Among these opposites that Fragment 67 speaks of, the
opposition between lack and satiety appears to be particularly
evident. We all know this experience, irrespective of any cosmological applications or explanations. What is enticing about
food presupposes hunger or perhaps appetite and disappears
with surprising suddenness when we are sated. The opposition
between war and peace is just as illuminating. The one is the
complete non-being of the other. The outbreak of war is a total
transformation of everything. Waking and sleep also belong in
this list. Indeed, what is so astounding about the opposition
between waking and sleep is also the suddenness with which
one entire condition becomes the other. Whoever falls or sinks
into sleep seems to be a completely different person and yet is
still the same person as the one who appears in wakefulness.
For that matter, all of these pairs of opposites could simply be
understood according to the pattern of waking and sleeping
(Fragment 88).

Now, admittedly, among the oppositions in Fragment 88
we also come across 'living and dead' and, further on, 'young and
old.' What is the reciprocity of abrupt change supposed to signify
here? Perhaps in some measure 'young and old' can be explained
as a change in perspectives, insofar as direct human experience
confirms for us that 'old' and 'young' are quite relative to each
other. A person can suddenly be young, and this does not just
mean that he feels rejuvenated. He really is young. Likewise,
one can all of a sudden look old. In this way, the Platonic formulation—that the same thing is both the one and the other at the
same time—would hold perfectly true. They are both within
the entity. Only its aspect changes. Moreover, we also come

across the dialectical play of 'young and old' in a series of relations in Plato's *Parmenides* (141a f., 152a f.).

The greatest difficulty for our interpretation that occurs in these testimonies is posed by the opposition between life and death. There is certainly something significant about the fact that this opposition does not occur at this point in Heraclitus as something particular but rather as one in a long list of similar pairs of opposites. This reminds us of the fact that the role of death and the corresponding understanding of death within the Christian cultural horizon to which we belong is an extremely unusual and extraordinary one. The extraordinary role of death in this tradition still has an effect even today, when religious backgrounds are waning considerably in the modern world and the Easter belief that death will be overcome through resurrection conveys the general consciousness of culture less and less. Even if we no longer embrace death in all its irrevocability and inconceivable terror through Jesus and the entire Christian message in light of the redemptive act of vicarious suffering that the crucifixion represents—even if, that is, we no longer embrace it as believers—it still is not so easy to be sufficiently conscious of the special place that death has in our European culture and its account of the soul—and this holds just as true when we look at the Heraclitus testimonies.

We can look at this as a classic example of what, in the problem-context of hermeneutics, I have called 'historically effective consciousness' [*wirkungsgeschichtliches Bewußtsein*]. Our own preconceptions are so deeply entrenched that they hinder us in our understanding of other cultures and historical worlds. To achieve a better understanding, we must try to become conscious of our own preconceptions. In the case of Heraclitus, this is rather difficult because the influence of late antiquity and early Christianity on the Heraclitus tradition, primarily from Hippolytus and Clement, directly obtrudes upon our own preconceptions and, to this extent, leads us astray. On the other hand, we must remain conscious of our own preconceptions even as we must protect ourselves from making premature identifications. Of course, greater difficulties do arise where we still have to deal with completely different cultural horizons and traditions. We have only to think of the distortion of the Vedanta by the Kantian, Schopenhauer.

Human sensibilities everywhere have ascribed an overarching significance to the experience of death. This certainly holds true, as well, for Greek popular religion, for the image of Hades, for instance, for the river of forgetting that separates the living from the dead, as these images are depicted in the Homeric epics. Similarly, the divine drama that Aeschylus brought to the stage in his reinterpretation of the Prometheus myth shows that death is a kind of living question for humanity. At root, all religions are answers to the riddle of death, whether the answer ensues from a cult of death or an oracular cult, or from other forms of belief in the soul or immortality. Even the idea of Hades still serves as an answer to the incomprehensible riddle of death. Of course, some myths connected with the names Orpheus and Eurydice, perhaps, or with Alcestis, or, in a certain sense, even with the figure of Büßer's Sisyphus, appear to mitigate the irrevocability of death. But even these myths recount precisely how this overcoming of death miscarries. Certainly, Greek popular religion, with its idea of Hades and the isle of the blessed, has in mind the enduring presence of the departed and even a reunion with them through *nekyia*.[55] And yet, even today the breathtaking sorrow of Greek burial paintings still touches us. In his *Phaedo*, Plato himself allows the child inside the man to speak, a child whose anxiety in the face of death can never be completely alleviated.

Still, in Heraclitus, something else is at issue: the sudden shift from death to life is associated with the sudden shift from life to death. We find nothing of the kind in the doctrine of Hades. With the Orphean and Pythagorean doctrine of the transmigration of souls and the reincarnation of the souls of the deceased into new (previously) lifeless bodies, we might well render a kind of reciprocal relationship between death and life understandable. But, in the end, of course, this depends exclusively on the question of whether the ones who are newly incarnated in this way regain the memory of their prior lives. Although this may be promised to the initiates of such a cult, there was no real counterpart in such religious movements—no more in the later Greek world than in Homer—to the overcoming of death in

55. [A magical rite though which the shades of the dead could be summoned from the underworld.]

the sense that we find in the Christian doctrine of the death and resurrection of Jesus Christ. We must understand the entire Greek cult of death, like we do other religions, as a kind of holding fast to life. The peculiarity of the Christian religion consists in the fact that, through it, in its faith in the Resurrection as the salvation from death through the vicarious suffering of Jesus, the terror of death is not supposed to be mitigated but rather completely accepted. "Christ is my life and death my gain." To this extent, the pre-Christian world, and thus the whole of the Greek world as well, is separated from Christianity by an insuperable boundary, which is, perhaps, what Novalis was describing in his "Hymns to the Night."

We also become conscious of how different the Christian religious experience of death is when we read, for instance, the first proof for the immortality of the soul that Plato puts into the mouth of Socrates in the *Phaedo* (70d ff.).[56] It is difficult for the modern reader to understand that in this text we are generally suppose to be able to infer the balance of death and life, of dying and returning, from the universal cycle of natural life. The rhythm of natural life seems, quite simply, incommensurable with an account of the human soul. Plato even points to this in the *Phaedo* when Cebes consents only hesitantly to the change from death to life (*phainetai*, 71e). Finally, there is something bewildering in this for us when it is supposed to follow from this line of reasoning in the *Phaedo* that the souls of the dead not only continue to exist (*einai*, 72e), but that, as it says in the text, the good who have died will have a better existence than the bad (72e). This inference is so absurd that modern philology has stricken this added stipulation as being inauthentic, even though the text has been handed down to us coherently. How, indeed, are we to understand that this is supposed to follow from the rhythm of natural life? At this point, we are more likely to make sense of the fact that a further proof follows in the *Phaedo* by means of which the periodicity of natural events is appended to the famous Socratic argument concerning *anamnesis*. But even here, we ask ourselves how this proof is supposed to be

56. See my study, "The Proofs of Immortality in Plato's *Phaedo*," in *Dialogue and Dialectic: Eight Hermeneutical Studies on Plato*, trans. P. Christopher Smith (New Haven: Yale University Press, 1980), 21–38. The German text was originally published in GW 6, 187–200.

a complement to the first. Of course, the soul in the first argument is something quite different from the soul that remembers itself. In any case, we might consider here the entire mediated horizon of the transmigration of the soul, which resonates even further in Plato, especially in Socrates' conversation with the two Pythagoreans. But it is decisively important to make clear that this has nothing to do with Heraclitus.

There can be no question of a transmigration of the soul in Heraclitus, whereas a Greek spiritual realm common to both natural life and the thinking being becomes recognizable in Plato. On the contrary, Heraclitus, with his bold oppositional pairs, is aiming directly at the paradox of the sudden shift. Heraclitus' idea, therefore, is far more radical. Here there is not, as there appears to be in Plato, a determinate entity, the soul, that conserves itself as an unchangeable thing even in its self-differentiated modes of appearance and in its altered abode within the body or in Hades.

At this point, it might be helpful to recall a significant little scene in the Platonic *Phaedo*. Here (103a ff.), an unknown person—a clue, in fact, upon which an extraordinary emphasis is laid—interrupts the Socratic line of reasoning that has introduced the exclusion of the opposites of life and death in order to prove the immortality of the soul. The anonymous person recalls that precisely this transition from the one to the other, the transition of opposites into each other, had indeed been asserted at an earlier point in the dialogue (namely, 70d ff.). Socrates also uses this opportunity to make it clear to his friend Cebes that when one thinks the opposites as such and has their mutual exclusion in mind, in this case the thinking of opposites has a different sense from when one says regarding any topic at all, a *pragma* (the soul, for instance), that something moves itself from one opposite toward the other. This, in fact, presupposes the pure thought, oppositionality as such, its being as an idea. It means that the opposites become differentiated from that in which they appear. In Aristotle, this is later called *hypokeimenon*, an idea that the early oppositional thinking of the Ionians, such as that of the Pythagoreans, was not conceptually aware of at all. Later on, in the *Philebus* (23d, 26d), Plato illustrates this as a shortcoming of those who came earlier by expressly introducing 'the third kind,' that of the measured (in addition to that of the measure).

Remembering Plato can help us to get some idea of Heraclitus' real question. Neither the Aristotelian analysis of the 'movedness' [*die Bewegtheit*] of nature, nor even the ideas of the hero cult or the doctrines of the mysteries conveyed by Homer and Hesiod correspond to Heraclitus' true intention. For him, it is a question of the paradox of sudden change and, along with it, the being-one of being [*das Einssein des Seins*]. What is life and what is death; what are the creation and the extinction of life? This is the riddle that Heraclitus ponders. He seeks the one in all oppositionality, and, in the one, he finds what is oppositional—in fire, the flame; in the *logos*, the soul; in the one, the true (*hen to sophon*). Plato will depict the great Parmenides leading the bewildered young Socrates in some bold games—that the one is in everything, and that even the ideas themselves are oppositional, they pass over into one another, and they are the one. This is how Plato can appropriate Heraclitus.

And so I have come to the conclusion that we ought not to refer here to particular ways of representing things. Something else comes into play with the identity thesis—the suddenness with which the appearance of things changes. This really brings the opposition between life and death to the fore. We must interpret the entire doctrine in precisely this way. Any mitigation of oppositionality—that of death and life, for instance—would contradict the entire tenor of the doctrine of opposites. The idea is far more radical. No one determinate entity—the soul, for example—lies within everything that lives as what is unchangeable behind a self-altering appearance. It is the mystery of the nature of being itself, the one wise thing, the truly divine, that nevertheless manifests itself in the sudden shift between death and life. Even death is like an abrupt shift in the appearance of being.

Thus, we should to try once again to follow the program of the proem and to recognize the unobserved truth in familiar experiences. If Fragment 62 talks about the idea that the gods 'live our death,' then this could mean that their being first emerges through our death. Their being articulates itself as what it is in view of our finality (and surely not because they behave as spectators, as Fink suggests[57]). Correspondingly, we could understand that, in living, we die their death, which means that the

---

57. See Martin Heidegger and Eugen Fink, *Heraklit*, Frankfurt am Main, 1970, p. 158 f.

immortals do not emerge for us as what they are as long as the security and certainty of life keep us spellbound. Once again, however, the truth would be that, through their changeability, both perspectives prove their nothingness and confirm the one, that which alone is the wise, as the true.

With this, the identity of numerous assertions about the changing aspect of things comes to light, the interpretation of which is not in dispute. Thus, we read, for example, "The ass prefers chaff to gold" (Fragment 9). Or, "Seawater is drinkable for fish and necessary for their life, for human beings it is unpalatable and deadly" (Fragment 61). Or, "The most beautiful ape is ugly compared to the race of human beings" (Fragment 82). Or, "The wisest of human beings looks like an ape in comparison to a god" (Fragment 83). Even statements such as Fragments 84a and 84b, "change rests" or "always to be challenged and oppressed by the same thing is tiresome," should be dissociated from all unsatisfactory mythical applications like the ones Plotinus proposes. They deserve no credence. He himself expressly says, *amelêsas saphê hêmin poiêsai ton logon.*[58] These are all negative correspondences to the identity of what is different, and they allow what is identical to be recognized in difference.

Fragments 24, 25, and 27 can be interpreted similarly. They hardly intend any sort of special Heraclitean doctrine about the dead and their prospective fates, or even a mystery wisdom that would be closed off to those who were uninitiated but which Heraclitus would have shared with all his fellow initiates. Rather, here too is it is a question of something lying out in the open, well known to all, yet which no one recognizes in its true significance. One example of something familiar to everyone is the exaltation of one who has fallen in war, 'on the field of honor' (*arêiphatous*, Fragment 24). He is like one suddenly transformed. Everyone honors him, everyone sees him differently, as exemplary, as transfigured. This is Heraclitus' insight and says absolutely nothing of any participation in the hero cult. At most, for him, this would have been a cultically derived example of the suddenness of such an abrupt change.

Similarly, there can be no bogus mysterious declarations of unforeseen experiences of the hereafter lying hidden within Fragment 27. Rather, he simply means by this that people have

58. *Enneads*, IV.8 [6]1, 15–16.

such a different stature after their deaths, they are so elevated, that during one's lifetime one would not have considered it possible.[59] Fragment 18 seems to express the same experience from the perspective of the human world: "When one does not hope, neither will one find the unhoped for."[60] It is thanks to hope that what takes place presents itself in a completely different way than we could expect, precisely because it was unforeseeable and seemed unreachable. Because there can be surprise, there may be fulfillment. The unhoped-for comes only to the hopeful.

That such an interpretation, up to the change in perspectives, affects the sense of these Heraclitean expressions, is somewhat confirmed by at least Fragment 53. This fragment, of course, speaks expressly of war, the father of all things: "It proves some to be gods, others human beings." The impotence and the power of the human being both emerge from this. For some, the fact that they are cowardly slaves emerges; for others, it is the fact that they are truly free.[61] Again, this means that what is already lying within each person simply emerges. War, the true god, does not just lie at the root of the most extreme opposites; rather it itself gives rise to the change in perspectives. It is what is common to all discord, the real *logos* behind what is different, within which things are seemingly able to show themselves. Thus, Fragment 80 says that war is, in fact, what is common to all; it is that from which no one can withdraw and which comes to all in equal measures.[62] Thus, in Heraclitus we can read that 'dikê,' that which is shared equally by all, and 'eris,' strife, are one (I prefer to read, *kai dikên kai erin*). The commonality of justice and the commonality of strife encompass everything. What is common to all is, in truth, one and the same. The continuation of the passage (which, by the way, Diels placed here quite correctly) corroborates this.[63] In this way, even the immortals are a particularization that does not

---

59. Fragment 27: *anthrôpous menei apothanontas hassa ouk elpontai oude dokeousin.*

60. Fragment 18: *ean mê elpêtai, anelpiston ouk exeurêsei.*

61. Fragment 53: *Polemos pantôn men patêr esti, pantôn de basileus, kai tous men theous edeixe tous de anthrôpous, tous men doulous epoiêse tous de eleutherous.*

62. Fragment 80: *eidenai de chrê ton polemon eonta xunon, kai dikên erin....*

63. Kahn (p. 205 f.) has shown quite nicely how Heraclitus surpasses

exist without mortals (Fragment 62). Evidently, by 'immortals,' Heraclitus does not mean the god of Fragment 67, the one in the multiplicity of its appearances. It looks more like Heraclitus (anticipating Plato in an example of bold enlightenment thinking) puts the traditional world of the gods in a reciprocal relationship with the world of human experience. Just as war manifests the power and impotence of human beings, so the power of the gods emerges in the failure of human beings and the impotence of the gods in their own well-being. It is almost even more paradoxical that the immortality won by the fallen comes to them through death!

From here on, I would like to pose the general question of whether not all of the statements about fame and immortality, like Fragments 24, 25, and perhaps even 27, aim at the transformation of the dead. It seems to me that even Fragment 29 is a confirmation of this: "The noble choose the one instead of all others." This is supposed to say, of course, that their nobility is precisely constituted by the fact that they actually follow in their lives what, according to Heraclitus, is the one true thing. Some of these interpretations may remain individually questionable, and a resonance of conventional religious ideas may nevertheless play a role here—however, the attempt that has been generally accepted until now, the attempt, that is, to turn Heraclitus, because of his mystical tone, into a logical interpreter of the wisdom of the mysteries, fails because Heraclitus demands the thinking of the one, and thereby wisdom, not from the initiated but from all human beings.

But how is all of this compatible with the fire cosmology? With this question we must not only keep Heraclitus' style and the characteristics Plato ascribes to him in mind, but we must also take into account the polemical references made to the Milesian doctrine. Certainly, the claim to paradoxical enlightenment that the proem puts forward was always related to the behavior of human beings as a whole. And yet it looks as though the matter

---

the Homeric and Archilochan statements on war. He also correctly hears in this a reference to the statement that introduces the whole text. However, I do not see echoes here of the Anaximander fragment, which is familiar to us only by chance. Here, of course, *dikê* does not come to the fore as violent punishment, as it does in Anaximander; instead, it comes into play as the common (*xunon*). This is what the clueless ones (*apeiroisin*) continually misunderstand.

takes a peculiar turn here. Even this new science must consequently be subordinated to a kind of enlightenment. If we have thus far followed the general drift of the proem and not presupposed anything that everyday human experience is not supposed to teach and, in fact, really does not teach, we must now ask ourselves how Heraclitus criticizes and incorporates his own insights into the whole of the new enlightenment that the Milesians (but also the Pythagoreans and men like Xenophanes) were propagating.

This does not signal an abandonment of our basic principle. For it is not special knowledge that he makes his theme, but rather a new way of seeing the world—that is, thinking the *logoi*. The meteorological process lies out in the open for everyone to observe. Everyone must also ask him- or herself to what extent the demythologizing of the mythical picture of the world and the reception of the cosmogonical schema make such questions as the one about the beginning inevitable, and whether such world-forming processes cannot become operative everywhere, over and over again. Later corpuscular theory and atomism as such thought this and thought that it was basically understandable for every thinking consciousness. By this, I mean that Heraclitus need not be seen at all as propagating Ionian cosmogony and converting it into a cosmology. Yet, he often makes overly naive observations or applications of this cosmology, which can only mean that references to cosmological things are of secondary significance for him. When Heraclitus refers to the cosmogonical knowledge of his Ionian neighbors, his intention does not seem to be to enter into a competition with the great investigators and discoverers from Miletus. In general, he is not claiming to pull together new knowledge from all over but, instead, to bring to light the truth that is concealed within all that is self-evident or otherwise familiar. This springs from the introductory statement, which plays directly with the paradox of a truth that is visible to all and yet is misunderstood everywhere. This is why we will surely not get very far with the interpretation of his fire cosmology as a 'cosmology.' The tortured attempts of the later doxographers to reconcile the traditional Heraclitus statements with a cosmological schema (or even with the doctrine of the elements introduced by Empedocles and worked out by Plato and Aristotle) cannot be encouraging.

This is a matter of a few cosmological statements of the most highly paradoxical form. There is, moreover, Fragment 30,[64] which seems to be unique in the whole of the early tradition of cosmological thinking. I do not think that we can see in this a reference back to Ionian cosmogony (as has been recently attempted)—as if the Ionians would have taught anything with their cosmogony other than precisely this: that no god and no human being established this world order. The first part of Heraclitus' statement sounds rather like a positive reference to the Ionian doctrine of *physis*. But something else in this proposition sounds definitely Heraclitean, and that is the emphasis on the idea that this ordering is the same one for all things (or of all things). If this part of the text is genuine, it reminds us of the cautionary expression about the unreason of human beings, who, like those who dream, construct their own individual worlds (see Fragment 89). Evidently, what is essential in this statement is obviously that the expectation of an unchanging order of the world should be attributed precisely to the most restless of all the elements, fire. That which (in Anaximander's vision of the world) ordinarily maintains the grand balance all by itself, that is, maintains measure, or perhaps produces measure over and over again, is imposed upon that which is eternally living, and this means the ever restless fire. This measure is depicted here as the self-igniting and the self-extinguishing of fire—a curious reciprocation between what has been measuredly ordered and what is explosively sudden. In this way, it is apparent that igniting and extinguishing symbolize precisely that which is sudden, which is what inspired Heraclitus' vision of the world. And yet it is just as doubtless that Heraclitus also presupposes the measuredness of all events and only wants to reinterpret this same thing. To that extent, it is not a question of resolving the alleged cosmology into simple symbolics. It is much more a question of discovering in Heraclitus a new response to the experience of the being of the whole. This seems to me to be what the riddle posed in Fragment 30 suggests.

---

64. Fragment 30: *kosmon tonde, ton auton hapantôn, oute tis theôn oute anthrôpôn epoiêsen, all' ên aei kai estin kai estai pyr aeizôon, haptomenon metra kai aposbennunemon metra.*

If we now turn to the further texts of Clement, we can hardly doubt that the subsequent statement, Fragment 31,[65] connects immediately to our statement ("fire's transformations..."). But then, the phrase *pyros tropai* carries the same unmistakably paradoxical tone that made the first statement appear to be a paradox. All things are the eruptions of restless fire. It thus has nothing to do with the sonorous Ionian occurrence of equilibrium in which all opposites pay respective penalties and compensation for their predominance.

Certainly, the solstice points in the course of the sun could also resonate with this insofar as all change—even the seasonal course of the sun—and all reversal have something sudden in them, as the Greek term *tropai* suggests. But, still, the connection with the preceding statement remains decisive. Therefore, the rest of the passage must be understood from there on: What happens in igniting and extinguishing? Kahn has remarked rightly that, in what follows, the atmosphere, the air, is missing,[66] which means that what was essential to Ionian cosmic wisdom and clearly provided its direct intuitive ground (in Thales and Anaximenes) was left out. It seems to me that he is also correct when he points out that the most extreme opposite to fire, the sea, is referred to here as its other. The earthly sea encounters the heavenly fire as its most extreme counterpart.

The 'ever-living' (*aeizôon*, Fragment 30) clearly belongs together with inflaming and extinguishing. This must form the guiding thread of the interpretation. Even if we keep at a distance all later distinctions among fire, light, and heat (distinctions that perhaps already approach the difference between the sensible and the spiritual and overtake them), it already becomes clear from the statement above that fire is not a visible element but, on the contrary, that which constantly transforms itself over and against all constancy. This is precisely its living essence, that it nonetheless is the one—as are all living things. Fire also flares up according to measure and is extinguished according to measure—just as, for example, the living rhythm of waking and sleeping.

65. Fragment 31: *pyros tropai prôton thalassa, thalassês de to men hêmisu gê, to de hêmisu prêstêr...*
66. Kahn, p. 139 ff.

Fire thus presents the universal structure of all being. Fragment 90[67] explains it best: "All things are interchangeable with fire and fire with all things"—which means fire as opposed to gold. And like in Fragment 88, all things transform themselves like fire; they flare up like a flame and sink together into extinction. "Fire, too, transforms itself when it is mingled with incense" (Fragment 67).

The emphasis is continually placed upon the one that is the true and the wise behind all supposed differences, whether these are now opposition and the transformation of opposites into one another or relativity and the sudden change of perspectives. The changeable itself is the one. I think the cosmological evidence of transformations, *tropai*, explains itself most easily this way. Perhaps, what this means here is not 'turning points' but actual 'transformations.' It is not a question of whether fire is everything that transforms, but rather the reverse, that fire is fundamental to it all—like the sun. Clement's insertions understand this to be the *logos* and God![68] So, to me, the insertion of 'transformations with the sea' (*prôton thalassa*) seems to be understandable only if we do not see in it an initial transformation of fire into water but rather a simple expression of the beginning as Ionian cosmology hit upon it. To that extent, the clarification that Clement appends to it with *sperma tês diakosmêseôs* is not really all that wrong.

Even as things proceed further, fire itself does not appear to be just a phase. Only when we resolve to interpret the fragment in this way, I think, does it become possible to understand the concluding passage for the first time. Evidently, it only says that fire is fundamental and not that fire transforms itself into earth and so comes out as something that is half earth, or that something that is half fire becomes wind when a hot wind comes up. Thus, it does not say that the sea becomes something that is half earth and half hot wind, but rather that the hot wind begins

67. Fragment 90: *pyros te antamoibê ta panta kai pyr hapantôn hokôsper chrysou chrêmata kai chrêmatôn chrysos.*

68. Clement, *Stromateis*, V 14, 104, 4: *dynamei gar legei, hoti (to) pyr hupo tou dioikountos logou kai theou ta sympanta di' aeros trepetai eis hygron to hôs sperma tês diakosmêseôs ho kalei thalassan, ek de toutou authis ginetai gê kai ouranos kai ta emperiechomena. hopôs de palin analambanetai kai ekpyroutai, saphôs dia toutôn dêloi....*

with the drying out of the land ('half-way,' so to speak). This is an experience, of course, that we all know. When a brooding heat lies across the land, it stays cooler by the sea. This is why the concluding passage handed down to us fits nicely in with this—the fact that, in the end, the sea inundates everything again, just as it was in the beginning. If Clement wants to interpret this reconstruction as *ekpyrôsis,* we must establish that nothing in the text speaks of this. The text says only that, in the end the sea inundates everything again. Are we suppose to think that Clement really found in the text the idea that everything ultimately becomes fire? And that he would inadvertently have forgotten to cite it? Indeed, we are trusting the words of the Church Fathers all too much if we believe in a lacuna in the text at this point just because Clement says, *saphôs dia toutôn dêloi.* The only thing in the transmitted Heraclitus text that could point in this direction would be *anathumiasis,* evaporation. The doxography tells us fantastic things about this. In the doxography, there are light and dark clouds over land and sea. The flaming basins of the stars fill themselves from out of the light clouds. The difference between day and night, even the solar eclipse, is supposed to be explainable by this process. All of this is suitably cloudy. Obviously, Diogenes' source found no clear ideas in this. Instead, it appears that *anathumiasis* was the single real fundament for these tedious constructions. In any case, this has nothing to do with the alleged world conflagration, the '*ekpyrôsis.*' Clement was obviously unable to draw upon anything in the text for his interpretation—otherwise, he would have done so.

The intuition that is fundamental to the entire text is most readily described by Simplicius' concept of the *drastikon* (the 'active')[69]—a kind of general answer of Aristotelian physics to the Ionians. The first thing that can be indicated about this is the eternal movedness. It is encountered just as much in the restless fire as in the restless primordial sea. The fact that the establishing of land seems like 'death' from this perspective, is quite understandable. In contrast to the restless life of the ocean, the fixed land is something dead. So it seems to me that Heraclitus, with his doctrine of fire, was inquiring into the background of Ionian cosmogony. It was not the transformations of water (Thales) or air (Anaximenes) but rather the transformations of fire that

69. See note 8, above.

this was describing. This is, in a manner of speaking, spoken in the transmitted text with a provocative emphasis. If we now consider how in this period *thalassa* is almost a collective noun for the liquid, the fluid, the flowing, the restless (*ho kalei thalassan*, Clement says), then the entire doctrine of flux falls easily into line.

From here on, there is still one last step to take. How the cosmic aspect of the fire doctrine—even though it may be understood metaphorically—connects itself to the Heraclitean assertions about the soul is certainly a difficult question. It should also be pointed out that the basic evidence for the doctrine of flux is cited by Eusebius alone because of his reference to the *psychê*, which is *aisthêtikê anathumiasis* (Fragment 12). The Stoic interpretation that brings together the doctrine of flux with the doctrine of the soul on the basis of its own doctrine of *pneuma*, seems to me to be an exceedingly unreliable source. Therefore, at this point I would rather proceed from those texts in which immediate observations are expressed, observations that permit Heraclitus' fire doctrine to come back into a material connection that by itself proceeds unequivocally toward 'the psychical.' For all that, one result of our skepticism about the doxography's cosmological schema is that, for Heraclitus, fire should not so much make understandable and describe the experience of the world, describe how something comes to be from something else; it is more a question of the real riddle that fire implies for thinking. In 'ontological' terms, the establishment of fire and the extinguishing of fire are equally puzzling. Where does it come from; where does it go? The extinguishing may, in fact, subside visibly (in embers and ashes), but where does it come from? What is this sudden flaming up? I think it is not so much that Heraclitus seeks an explanation for this here, but that he recognizes in it the entire mystery of the *aeizôon*. To position fire as one element among the 'other' elements is, after all, an absurd paradox. It is the living essence itself, which makes itself manifest as restless self-movement. The real riddle of being is not how the same ordering of the whole maintains itself in the change of events, but that the being of this change even takes place. Heraclitus understood this as the one within all opposites—the unity of what is under tension in the opposites. This confirms Plato's unambiguous expression in which he contrasts the 'tense Ionian' muses with the 'Sicilian' ones. At the same time, this also describes the structural law of those statements that we would like to associate with Heraclitus on the basis of their family resemblance. The 'one wisdom' of Heraclitus is not how the one passes over into the other, but that the one is also the other without any transition. Without transition, suddenly, like lightning—one comes to the puzzling *exaiphnês* in Plato's *Parmenides* (156d)[70] in a sense that finds no proper place in the Eleatic antitheses, just like *metapesonta* (Fragment 88).

The spatial term for such a transitionless otherness is 'touching together' (*haptesthai*)—the key word in the profound Fragment 26: "The human being kindles a light in the night, when the eyes are extinguished. Alive, he touches the dead; awake, he touches the sleeping."[71] The statement poses many riddles. As anyone who has ever lit candles on a Christmas tree knows, there is a close semantic relationship that exists between the two meanings of *haptein*, 'to kindle' and 'to touch.' If one holds the igniting candle even just a little off to the side, it will not light the other one. 'To ignite' means 'to touch.' How far these two meanings play into each other is obviously the question—so much so, in any case, that there can be no talk of a play on words at all, even if the middle voice, *haptetai*, is not generally used transitively.

Nevertheless, the tradition provides a clear hint in Clement. It is a question of the correspondence between sleep and death. He speaks of the *apostasis tês psychês*, which is greater in death than it is in sleep. If we proceed from here, then we can easily understand: "Living, he touches the dead. Awake, he touches the sleeping." Is, for instance, *heudôn* ('when he sleeps') supposed to have been added by Heraclitus as a solution for poor riddle solvers? The style of the polarities would be perfect without this addition, and the solution—taking its departure from the last word—would be easy enough. We understand this. Waking and sleeping, life and death, immediately touch one another. To apply a concept that I can not yet find evidence of in Plato, waking is a *metabolê* (even though in colloquial Greek its usage

70. See my study, "Der platonische 'Parmenides' und seine Nach-wirkung," in *Plato im Dialog*, GW 7, 322 ff.
71. Fragment 26: *anthrôpos: en euphronêi phaos haptetai heautôi [apothanôn] aposbestheis opseis: zôn de haptetai tethneôtos heudôn [aposbestheis opseis], egrêgorôs haptetai heudontos.*

is perfectly ordinary—for the weather, for example, like 'Umschlag' in German). There is no transition between sleeping and being awake. Either one is 'here' or one is not 'here'—in consciousness, that is. The phenomena that Heraclitus has in mind are such 'total' opposites that they show themselves to be one precisely through the suddenness of the shift from the one into the other. The waking one and the sleeping one are one and the same, the one who 'is alive.' Moreover, when one sleeps, one exists differently; in a puzzling way, one is not 'there'; one is like a dead person; and we even say of one who is fast asleep that he sleeps 'like the dead.' There is something mysterious in the suddenness of the shift, when, all of a sudden, the one who falls asleep is 'gone.' This also holds true for the beginning of the 'sleep of death,' although this is a conclusive shift. To me, so far, this epigrammatically abbreviated text not only seems to sound Heraclitean, but it even seems to be worthy of Heraclitus. In being awake and being sleep, in something that anyone can observe at any time without thinking anything of it (*apeiroisin eoikasi peirômenoi*), he apprehends 'the one wise thing' (*hen sophon*) of death and life.

But, what is the first statement of the fragment trying to say (*anthrôpos haptetai...*)? Certainly, the fact that human beings 'master' fire and make light by themselves is one of the oldest experiences of humanity, an experience that found its expression in the myth of Prometheus. It is also certain that igniting or lighting a fire is still something marvelous. We also understand how the lighting of candles or an oil lamp demonstrates the sameness of what is burning and what can burn in such a way that everything is fire.

But is this all there is to it—a correspondence of natural extinguishing and self-igniting with sleeping and waking, a correspondence of death and life with the 'art' of using fire? Clement cites the whole thing for the sake of waking and awakening and generally has in view the Christian faith in resurrection that comes from the promise of Christianity. To this end, the obviously authentic proposition from Heraclitus must have been remolded somewhat so that the statement, *anthrôpos en euphronêi phaos haptetai eautôi*, is to be understood either in a Stoic sense or as having been forced by Clement into a Christian connection with the help of the insertion of *apothanôn*. This permits the Christian author to recognize in *euphronê* (the 'well-meaning') not only a kind of semantic testimony of participation in *phronêsis* ('contemplation') but nothing short of a kind of semantic testimony of faith in the Resurrection.

But how did Heraclitus himself connect the concluding passage, the analogy between life and death, waking and sleeping, to the first statement? That 'the human being' itself kindles a light in the night already points to a very particular use of fire: 'to make light.' This does not fit the situation of the sleeper. To me, it also seems misguided to relate such a general assertion about 'the human being' to the dream life, as many interpreters assume at this point in view of the *aposbestheis opseis*. As if we could master our dreams like the fire we light—then the emphasis of 'by himself' (*heautôi*) would be unintelligible! To be sure, Heraclitus does often oppose the worlds of dreams and delusion to the common world of the day and reason. Yet, in the event that the addition, *aposbestheis opseis*, is really to be retained (and, in any case, it does point toward 'igniting' by means of its semantic contrast with 'extinguishing'), it must have a special point. The 'extinguished eyes'—if this actually occurs in Heraclitus' original statement—necessarily give the night a metaphorical sense. The night in which we do not dream but instead see, thanks to the light that we ourselves kindle—this is what we all do when 'the human being' awakens! The real peculiarity of 'the human being' is not the dreaming but the dawning of this inner light that we call thinking or consciousness (see, for instance, Fragment 116[72]). Now, whether the addition of *apobestheis opseis* is really Heraclitean or has been added as a solution guide by a good advisor on Heraclitean riddles—it suits the meaning.[73]

Thus, we receive unexpected reinforcement from this for thinking inflaming, self-movement, and the 'soul' together. Whatever else *psychê* might have been in early Greek thought, the list of assertions that Heraclitus makes here about the 'soul'

---

72. Fragment 116: *anthrôpoisi pasi metesti ginôskein heôutous kai sôphronein.*

73. Uvo Hölscher (*Anfängliches Fragen*, Göttingen: Vandenhoeck & Ruprecht, 1968, p. 156–160) looks at the matter from the same angle but, in my opinion, still takes the 'physics of the soul' too literally—but then, again, not literally enough—when he completely dissociates the literal sense of 'to touch' from *haptein*, a sense which is indispensable in the opening clause.

forces us to see in *psychê* not just the living something that escapes with the dying breath. The Socratic/Platonic resonances are unmistakable, even if Pythagoras and his idea of *anamnesis* as the path to salvation from the cycle of births may have already been playing a role there.

Let us assume that what is meant here is not the light of the dream but rather the brightness that we call 'consciousness,' and this is indeed really like an abrupt awakening from sleep, a 'coming to oneself' (*heautôi*!). Then the Heraclitean *logos* gains its full expressive power for the first time: the *pyr phronimon* that flames up when one comes 'to oneself' (and this takes a while for some sleepers!) is no isolation but the path toward participation in the common day and the common world. It is obtained in *phronein* and *logos* but obviously lost in madness as well.

Thus the whole of the Heraclitean doctrine is connected to the profundity of these analogies and parallels in which fire and soul, water and death are so peculiarly enclosed; and yet, at the same time, these assertions break through the enclosure of these entwinements and thereby assume an appealing character and exhort us toward insight.

Admittedly, some of these exhortative passages hardly seem to correspond to the morphological criteria for genuine Heraclitean style from which I am proceeding. But is this not perhaps more often due to the trivializing citations? I offer an example in which the excavation of such a trivializing can be demonstrated in two steps. This is Fragment 46: *tên te oiêsin hieran noson elege kai tên horasin pseudesthai*, "Self-deluding, he called epilepsy, and seeing, he called deceptive." Today, it is acknowledged that we must filter out the assertion about *oiêsis* from the epistemological context in which it appears here. We must restore the word's original moral sense, which has nothing to do with Plato's *doxa*.[74] It seems to me that no proof is needed for the

---

74. Thus, the word is encountered in Fragment 31 in the understanding that is to be expected here: (*elege tên*) *oiêsin prokopês egkopên*—and, moreover, in the most genuinely gnomic style. And, elsewhere, it is referred to as 'old': Johannes Damascus, *Sacra* par. 693e (see Mondolfo/Tarán, *Eraclito. Testimonianze e Imitazioni*, Florence: La nuova Italia, 1972, p. 221 ff.). See also, for instance, Euripides Fragment 270: *dokêsis*, which is similar to Heraclitus' Fragment 17, *dokeousi*. This, of course, does not substantiate the use of the word *oiêsis* (and Corpus Hippocrates, IX, 230, *Littré* is also not an actual testimony.)

fact that the epistemological use of the word in Plato (*Phaedo*, 92a, *Phaedrus*, 244c) is not its original use (see Euripides, Fragment 643). On the contrary, in Homer the pragmatic meaning of *oiomai*, 'to foresee,' suggests that we understand *oiêsis* as 'madness,' delusional self-certainty, blind optimism. From there, one's own self proves itself to be the favorite object of delusional self-certainty.

Oiêsis, therefore, corresponds to self-esteem. Does Heraclitus then really want to make cold-hearted fun of epilepsy when he compares it to *oiêsis*? If we keep in mind the exact expression for epilepsy that had become the 'technical' one, 'the sacred illness,' we should not put too much weight on the 'fallen ones' as such. Rather, the 'sacred illness' of epilepsy connotes a devout awe and forbearance for those afflicted by it. For one to rob or otherwise harm one who has fallen from it would be nothing less than a sacrilege.

I think, then, that Heraclitus wants to say something important here. The moment of awe and forbearance is also suited to the opinion that all human beings have of themselves. An element of madness, of blind self-indulgence, lies within every human. We might call it a sickness. To get over it through self-critique and reason, with the help of that reason that is common to us all, would lead to a proper, healthy self-esteem. Nevertheless, this 'sickness'—so far as it is one—demands a certain forbearance. No one can bear to be without an opinion of himself (even a modest one). In *Lord Jim*, Joseph Conrad has described the tragic life of a young man who, through guilt, has suffered the complete loss of this opinion of himself.

This paradoxical statement certainly does not intend to exhort forbearance for illusions about ourselves. But Heraclitus sees the power of the illusions that each of us has about ourselves—just as he correctly sees that human fate is not stamped upon us by the divine guidance of a 'daimon' but rather by the proper guidance of life ('ethos'); he even says this in Fragment 119: *êthos anthrôpôi daimôn*. Why shouldn't both the calamity of madness and the dictates of forbearance occur in Heraclitus? They could have occurred here (Fragment 43 with Fragment 46 appended to it): *hubrin chrê sbennunai mallon ê pyrkaiên: tên de oiêsin hieran noson elege....*

Perhaps this is the case. Like so much else, it would certainly accord with the profound vision of that connoisseur of the soul, Heraclitus. We cannot mistake the fact that his style of thinking is far more closely associated with the pregnancy and sharpness of gnomic aphoristic wisdom than it is to Ionian science. The critical confrontation with the latter, which is expressed in the doctrine of fire, gives rise to astounding assertions about the 'psychê' and its 'logos.' The idea that the *logos* of the soul 'increases itself'[75] must—I think—be seen, along with all of the assertions that emphasize the one unity hidden behind what is oppositional, as the 'one wise thing.' We may not presuppose here, in a post-Cartesian way, the 'substantial' distinction between an outer and an inner—we must recognize the simplest observation in this, the observation that the *psychê* is 'life' and that the living, in distinction to everything, is the total that becomes more because something is added to it; it enlarges 'itself,' unfolds 'itself,' moves 'itself,' and, in the end, it seeks 'itself.' This 'itself,' which suffuses all 'abrupt change' with one and the same thing, places Heraclitus in opposition to the Milesian thinking on opposites. The self-igniting of fire, the self-moving of the living, the coming to itself of the waking one, and the self-thinking of thinking, are all manifestations of the one *logos* that always is. The mysterious 'itself' is what accounts for all of Heraclitus' profundity. Here, in an inimitable way, he maintains that unique middle that, in modern thinking, has gotten lost in the reflexivity of self-consciousness: *haptetai heautôi*. Is it igniting—'for itself'?—or is it becoming inflamed 'by itself,' like a log in the fireplace? Not to know this is the 'lone wise thing.'

From this we understand how the Platonic question of the one and the many can recognize itself again itself in the 'tense' muses of Ionia. It seems that Heraclitus' vision is a synopsis of being alive, being conscious, and being. It was precisely this task of thinking together what has thus been separated that Plato saw himself confronted with. The *Phaedo* vividly tells this story, which begins with the natural principle of the 'soul,' the principle that there can, of course, be no 'life' without the arc of the natural cycle. This is why nature renews life over and over in a rhythmic return—so that there is no death for it. This, however, is but one aspect of life and soul. There is also *the* life, for which death is something because a human being is something other

---

75. Fragment 115: *psychês esti logos heauton auxôn*.

than just a link in the chain of life that rolls rhythmically on. Life has memory; so through 'experience' it becomes more, it increases 'itself' by traveling through the circular course of life. This is the thinking that the *Phaedo* enacts. Socrates shows his friends how the principle of life and these other principles of 'thinking' and 'anamnesis' are one and inseparable in just the same way that becoming and being are. (Anaxagoras knew better than to unify them.)

In the *Phaedrus*, the myth of the ascent of the soul and its downfall embodies this same insight. Here, Plato fashions and inspires his Socrates as a true master of poetic discourse and speculative irony who makes his young friend, who was thoughtlessly heeding rhetorical virtuosity, conscious of the fact that *eros* is something other than the calculus of profit and pleasure that Lysis' artful piece of rhetoric imagines. But before this flood of mythic imagination begins to run its breathtaking course, Socrates puts forward something like a proof: "All soul is immortal"; and, "all that is soul concerns itself with that which is soulless."[76] Notice here that 'soul' suddenly becomes the principle of self-movement! The story that is then told recounts that this principle, which holds sway throughout the entire universe and through which the heavens obtain their order, also has its place in the soul of the individual and indeed in the unity of 'loving' and 'learning.' Insofar as 'learning' is 'anamnesis,' the remembrance of the true, each of us has a share of what is true. This is obviously the great insight that Plato is alluding to here—which, at this point, he calls *apodeixis* (245c 4). Self-movement is truly a miracle. While everything in motion is usually moved by something and is in motion only so long as it is moved, that which is living, that which has a soul, is in motion by its own impetus and is in motion as long as it is alive. This has its own evidence. This evidence is strong enough to derive yet another proof for the immortality of the soul. The world, this great ordering composed of astral and earthly movements, cannot be bound at all to the idea of a state of rest. Socrates concludes the following from this: that which is the cause of such self-movement, the soul, must always be there as well. It looks as though Plato, at this point, fulfills an expectation that, as it says

---

76. *Phaedrus*, 245c 5: *psychê pasa athanatos*; 246b 6: *psychê pasa pantos epimeleitai tou apsychou*.

in the *Charmides* (196a), "only a very wise man" could fulfill, namely, to show that there is a *dynamis* that moves on its own and not by virtue of something else. At the same time, he would also show himself to be the Delian diver who brought something precious to light from out of the dark depths of Heraclitus.

In this way, Plato is interpreting the being of the human being in the great scope of cosmic events in that he unifies the two aspects of self-movement and 'logos' in mythical metaphors. Aristotle sought to perfect this unification in his conceptual constructs (*kinêsis, noêsis, energeia*),[77] and Hegel, that great Aristotelian of modernity, follows him. However, is Heidegger not also justified when he discovers a Heraclitus who is inquiring back behind metaphysics, yet one in whom all things play into one another? Could he not also have discovered Plato's dialectic, in which the play of these ideas is played out further?

77. He also refers to Heraclitus for this: *De Anima*, A 2, 405a 25–28: *to de kinoumenon kinoumenôi ginôskesthai*. However, Heraclitus is also co-intended at 405a 5 (*tisi pyr*).

3
Ancient Atomic Theory

In the time of the unrestrained triumphal march of modern scientific explanation the relationship of natural scientific research to its history was a peculiarly indifferent one. It viewed its own history under the guiding idea of an advancement in research. But this means that the always contemporary position of research contains within itself everything that has ever been acquired in the history of this science with respect to positive knowledge. A position vis-à-vis the history of this research can merit attention, therefore, only from out of an interest subordinated to the interests of historical research in general. According to its own conception of things, for science itself to investigate the natural-scientific worldview of an earlier time remained an indifferent undertaking—a worldview that did not yet have this or that knowledge and therefore suffered under misapprehensions that have since been overcome. Admittedly, historical scientific scholarship could occasionally present current research with a stimulating impetus, provided that the problems that had occupied a past epoch of research came to light again in a fresh way, one that was interesting for the present. But such cases were actually not only extremely rare, but, above all, because of the notion that the present position of science already had in its keeping all of the problems that its objects had ever posed for it, these historical cases could present no real impetus for an interest in historical research. Whenever science did turn back toward the extraneous historical work of such a task, it was only an inadvertent forgetfulness of its proper task.

Now, undoubtedly, the delimitation of classical mechanics by the discoveries of the latest physics has brought about a certain easing of this situation. The necessity of relinquishing seemingly certain fundamentals of classical science in the fields of nuclear physics and astrophysics facilitates the possibility of yet seeing the origination of this classical science from perspectives other than that of the advances that it has achieved, which means, however, that it also facilitates the fundamental possibility of seeing in modern natural science a historically determined aspect—one whose intellectual and ideological meaning is not fully determined by the pure attainment of knowledge.

The research itself, which in this way seems to come to the aid of an historical examination of classical science, is nevertheless far from drawing such conclusions for its own sense of itself. Rather, it sees in its new achievement a self-evident operation of its fundamental principle—that of overcoming errors in scientific progress and preserving only the truths. Thus it awards to classical mechanics ancient, undisputed validity within the domain of its own boundaries, and—with its abandonment of Euclidian space and the idea of complete causal determination, in addition to its demonstration that the intuitive model of the atom is no longer tenable—the new scientific research believes itself to have refuted not so much Newtonian science as the *interpretation of it through the philosophical apriorism of the intuition.*[1] Indeed, the logical consistency of this positivistic self-interpretation corroborates itself in the consistency of the progress of research from classical mechanics to the new physics. We would be misjudging the situation, however, if we were to discern that this forward development of natural science had itself simply taken a wrong turn. The significance of this revolutionary development of the newest physics lies precisely in the fact that it makes its basic principles obvious and thereby forces philosophical consciousness to take up the question of the ontological meaning, the intellectual presuppositions, and the claim of this knowledge of nature in their full weight. A

1. [*den philosophischen Apriorismus der Anschauung.* Among other things, 'Anschauung' can mean both 'intuition' and 'perception' in the physical sense. I have translated it both ways, depending on the context (though mostly as 'intuition'); but in most contexts making a hard and fast distinction between the two senses would be inappropriate.]

mathematizing of nature, whose origins lie in the centuries in which modern natural science has developed itself into the essential determining factor of modern culture, perfects itself in the fundamental abandonment of intuitiveness, which seems to have become inevitable, certainly not for the practice of the individual physical sciences, but for the theoretical interpretation of their collective results.

Thus, even now, it is definitely not the interests of natural science itself that induce it to take an interest in its history. Scientific research as such would have no scruples about absolving itself from the intuitiveness of the field of the astronomical and atomic events it explores if it were not thereby pressed to admit that this new knowledge is in no way more capable of transforming the natural worldview of the intuition. Of course, Newtonian science also had to relinquish broad areas of natural events that an essentially descriptive process of contemplating nature reserves to itself because such events exceeded the possibilities of mechanical-causal explanation. But this did signify a real transformation of the natural worldview under the causal-mechanistic mode of perception that attained the fundamental power of its expression in the existence [*Dasein*] of technology. Its spiritual meaning and its significance for the whole of human life were by themselves comprehensible to everyone. The new turn against this led to conceptual consequences that severed this self-evident connection. Something like an 'empirical philosophy'[2] would hardly suffice to reconstitute this connection, nor would it be suitable. So it is no coincidence that a historical interest in its own heritage is emerging, an interest that belongs within the context of its own mode of interpretation and touches upon its essential basis as a science. No one today can say whether this task of interpretation will not one day help to determine the course of scientific advancement itself.

The beginnings of modern natural science are widely thought to be determined by the productive adoption and further development of ancient ideas, a process through which the fundaments of the dominant Aristotelian/Medieval view of nature were destroyed. Among these ancient ideas, the *idea of the atom*

2. See the journal *Erkenntnis, zugleich Annalen der Philosophie* (1930 ff.) (and the movement for the 'unity of science' that was spreading around the world in the meantime).

occupies a particularly prominent position. In their reawakening, the interests of incipient scientific research and critical exposition allied themselves with the Christian worldview and the science of the 'School.' The main source of ancient atomism, the didactic poem on the nature of things by Lucretius, who was accused of heresy because of his atheism, was among the most powerfully effective books of this time. We possess a thorough and clear-sighted depiction of the significance of ancient atomism for the emergence of the modern natural sciences in Kurt Lasswitz's great work, *The History of Atomism*.[3] This depiction, however, lacks an interpretation and assessment of ancient atomism itself—and not for incidental reasons. The philosophy of the modern natural sciences, which provided the systematic guiding thread for Lasswitz's historical research, also posited a temporal limit for this same research. He interprets the natural philosophy of antiquity only insofar as it is relevant to incipient modernity. The historical attitude of this philosophical historian of atomism is demonstrate in the fact that he stays within the limits set for him by the guiding idea of a progress in the conceptual methods of natural scientific research.

In fact, the picture that modern historical research paints of ancient atomism is determined most informatively by the undisputed validity of the scientific ideal of the modern natural sciences. This expresses itself in a remarkable insecurity about its historical value, which in turn leads to a corresponding insecurity about the actual doctrine of ancient atomism. As is well known, we possess no original overall interpretation of ancient atomism from its actual scientific heyday (from the fifth to the fourth century before Christ) but only from the scientifically fatigued period of Hellenistic Epicureanism. The countercurrents to ancient atomism that had come to prevail in Aristotle's natural philosophy now determine the peculiar doctrine of Epicurean natural philosophy so completely that they distort its picture of the original atomism of Democritus and Leucippus in essential points.[4] Thus we can only recognize in them one

3. Reprinted by the *Wissenschaftlichen Buchgesellschaft*, Darmstadt 1963.
4. I think, above all, of the doctrine of the falling of atoms, for instance, which, supported by the authority of Eduard Zeller, has long fooled scholarship and has been clarified by A. Goedeckemeyer. See,

source for the reconstruction of the original atomism—and not a particularly excellent source at that. The open opposition of Aristotle is therefore more reliable for us than this spasmodic adherence and its exponents in late antiquity. But this is precisely the point where the historical view was biased by the fact that this ancient opponent of atomism has been, at the same time, the great vanquished adversary of early modern natural science. Thus, in the collision of this collective opposition against Aristotle, historical research has pulled ancient atomism into line with modern natural science and for this reason has been inclined many times to reconstruct a system for explaining nature from the sparse accounts of the ancient ones—a system that already contained the basic principles of modern natural science.

From out of this historical observation, however, arose the reverse question of why this futuristic attitude of ancient natural science has been attributed to Aristotelean philosophy for two thousand years. And if one did not want to use the evasive excuse that the ancient intellect had simply become too tired to develop modern natural science from out of these rudiments of ancient atomism all by itself, one had to look for internal shortcomings in these rudiments. This happened again, however, in the sense that one measured ancient atomism on the scale of progress from out of which modernity took its seemingly identical foundation. Thus, we have seen the historical impossibility of a further fruitful development of ancient atomism in the shortcomings of its accomplishments—for instance, in its lack of a mechanics of colliding bodies. Or, on the other hand, we have trusted in the authority of Aristotle to the extent that, considering the state of the knowledge of nature at that time, we have conferred upon his physics a real priority over the atomistic—for this future first arose from out of the developed state of the mathematical/physical methods of modern times.

Thus, the estimation of ancient atomism fluctuates between the extreme contrasts of an unreserved admiration for its prospective modernity and a confident devaluation of its scientific and philosophical weight. This evaluative fluctuation corresponded to the conception and reconstruction of the doctrine itself. We can be permitted to suppose that neither opposition befits the true

Geodeckemeyer, "Epikurs Verhältnis zu Demokrit." Straßburg (Dissertation) 1897.

situation. But we can find a real settlement of this controversy only from a new ground that replaces the common standard, the standard against which it has been measured until now. But this common standard is the idea of modern natural science, before which this atomism may stand or fall. If we elaborate it in such a way that it stands up to modern science, then the philosophy of Aristotle is a Scholastic error; if we keep it on the footing of its factual knowledge of nature so that it fails, then Aristotle's philosophy is the relatively superior (albeit superseded) point of view, which the decree of its historical success confirms. Now, at the moment we are ready to direct our gaze toward the historical uniqueness and the intellectual presuppositions of the modern mathematical natural sciences, we will have to withdraw ourselves at the same time from the standard they offered for evaluating ancient atomism and build ourselves an image of that ancient 'natural science' from out of what it was within the whole of Greek natural *philosophy* and as a complete interpretation of nature and existence.

Ancient atomism is not a research hypothesis of a mathematical/physical science that would have to prove itself by achieving an exact explanation for the reality of experience and that claimed validity only as far as it was indispensable for this explanation and the interpretation of experimental data. It is, rather, a basic sketch of true reality as it grows out of the philosophical question of the being of reality.[5] Thus, it belongs within the context of the dawn of Greek philosophy, which seeks to think the thoughts of *nature*. The mythological worldview that understood the events in nature and the fates of human beings from out of the decrees and active intervention of the reigning gods faded with the first thinking of these events. It is extremely significant that we attribute the saying, "Everything is full of gods" (that is, that the powers that determine natural events and the existence of human beings in nature lie within nature itself), to Thales, the man whom we consider to be the first philosopher. When Democritan atomism reinterpreted this saying in the form of a 'shocking atheism' (as it were) and explained everything entirely on the basis of that ultimate invisible reality of swarming

---

5. This is admittedly true of some forms of the atomism of later times as well. See Lasswitz 1, 401 ff., this is a significant fact for explaining the metaphysical presuppositions of the modern natural sciences.

atoms, it was only thinking this conception of nature through to its logical conclusion.[6] From Thales to Democritus, the 'sages' are searching for the answer to the question of what nature is: What is it that is permanent in this continual flux of occurring and passing away that grants it rules and order and reliable recurrence? None of the answers that the 'physicists' gave for this question is a 'physical' thesis in the sense of the modern natural sciences. Whenever the physicists adopted one or more materials, either within then or outside of their operative forces, forces that form the contours of the world from these materials, an intuition of the true essence of reality always guided them, and they availed themselves of the 'natural scientific' knowledge from which they proceeded in a peculiarly free mode of analogical generalization. This is important for the question of the essence and purpose of atomism. Indeed, there is a vast difference between those oldest theories of matter, which found the multiplicity of appearances indicated in the condensation and rarefaction of a basic material, and the 'scientific' theory of atomism, which first made the phenomena of condensation and rarefaction genuinely explicable. And yet it will be shown that even the atomism of an original overall interpretation of being was guided by a rational explanation and not by the sheer effort to fortify those half-mythical material doctrines of the Ionian philosophers.

Admittedly, what seems to give ancient atomism its particular priority within Greek natural speculation is the radicalness with which it attributes the entire world of qualities to the bare form and movement of the atoms. The fact that this theory looks suspiciously like an anticipation of kinetic gas theory will always make it interesting to the present-day naturalist. But the historian will also see the summit and perfection of the Greek enlightenment in it because it is far superior to all other contemporary corpuscular theories in its simplicity and rationality. Although certainly the proximity to the atomistic worldview is to be recognized in Empedocles' doctrine of the elements—especially his explanation of sense perception by 'pores' and 'effluences'[7]—and in Anaxagoras' qualitative atomism, still, they have precisely missed the chilling consequences with which atomism

6. See Diels, VS 55 A 74, 78.
7. See Walter Kranz, *Empedokles und die Atomistik*, Hermes 1917.

excludes all qualitative differences from the primary realities of being and all intellectual forces from the concept of the natural order. Thus the worldview of an Empedocles or an Anaxagoras is less of a mediating precursor to the atomic theory of Leucippus and Democritus than were some of the rather less coherent ways of playing out the enlightenment inclinations of the time. By their proximity, however, they let us see the audacity of atomic theory, only more so—the audacity, that is, with which this theory undertook to explain, from one single basic assumption, all forms of natural occurrence: the coming into being and passing away of nature [*Wesen*], growth and decay, qualitative change and change in location.[8] Indeed, when we look at the rationality of this ancient atomism we want to call upon this precursor to confirm the correctness of modern natural science. But we will have to ask ourselves whether the basic precepts of the Greek conception of the world would not be violated here and whether a foreign (as well as distant) future conception of a plenum would prematurely announce the end of the Greek understanding of existence.

The following arguments will try to show that this is in fact so and that the grounds for the overthrow of ancient atomism are situated precisely within atomism itself. Along with the specifically Greek conception of the order of nature that is also operative in it, the interpretation of the world by means of an atomistic mechanics enters into an inner tension that paralyzes it and leads it into the proximity of skepticism. First, the alienation of the presuppositions of Greek ontology in the beginnings of modernity opens the idea of the atom for its triumphal progress in the *mathematical* sciences.

The decisive step that Leucippus and Democritus took—the assumption of emptiness as an internal structural element of the corporeal world—is a radical break with natural intuition and the philosophical concept of the body. To assume empty space exterior to the whole of the corporeal world is obviously something quite natural, and the idea that wherever a body changes its location there must be empty space is just as natural and nearly as intuitive (even if the philosophers have not been able to think this intuition) as having a location for self-movement. But, in addition to this, the Democritan theory, which conceived the

8. See, Aristotle, *On Generation and Corruption*, I 2.

corporeal itself as an accumulation of indivisible particles per-
meating empty space, was, of course, in no way contradictory
to previous philosophical conceptions of corporeal being. Admittedly, this assumption of emptiness could make phenomena
truly comprehensible: change of location, condensation and rarefaction, growth, and so on. But how that emptiness could be
something that exists, and even something that constantly and
necessarily belongs to the being of physical things—that was
difficult to think through by means of the Greek concept of
being that had been formulated in the philosophy of Parmenides.
The history of more recent natural science confirms that oppositions rooted in the substance concept of Greek ontology opposed
the recognition of a vacuum. The production of the macroscopic
vacuum in Torricelli's experiment first cleared the path that the
ancient objections to the existence of the vacuum had either
kept obstructed or had been permitted to follow only hesitantly
and only for microscopic vacua (e.g., by Galileo in his *Discorsi*).

In fact, to this day, the atomistic thesis that both emptiness
and a plenum exist has not yet been thought through in its ontological consequences. The mode of being of a mathematical
sketch as it represents empty space is also an unexplicated ontological problem in more recent philosophies of nature; so even
mathematical physics was naturally accustomed to relying on the
being of the *spatium absolutum* before it became required in
the course of the most recent research for positing the basic
givens of mathematical nature—givens that are in complete
ontological suspension.

Which ones, then, are the fundamental assumptions upon
which the worldview of ancient atomism are based? The answer
to this question points most clearly to how very much ancient
atomism remained determined by the ontology that impressed
itself upon the idea of substance. With its assumption of emptiness, it does not venture into the dimension of mathematical
abstraction; rather, it undergirds the reality of sensual experience
by a true world of things and processes that possesses a peculiar
intuitiveness, albeit one withdrawn from our observation. Like
all Greek natural philosophers before Aristotle, the Atomists
presented their philosophy in the form of an origin of the universe
(a cosmogony).[9]

9. For this explanation of atomistic cosmogony we can thank

The beginning of world formation contains no assertion concerning the motive force that gives rise to it. There is emptiness and fullness in the universe. This universe is limitless with respect to space and time. World formation occurs when many multiform corpuscles are discharged from out of the infinite, the borderless reserve, as it were, of all world becoming and move into the great emptiness. When they collide and conglomerate, they generate a quaking vortex that, as in a winnowing fan, brings like together with like, the larger accumulations that have gathered sinking toward the center from where they expel the light, fine atoms, which scatter into the great void until a globule forms, which in turn pulls a kind of crocheted network of atoms around itself like a skin—the beginning of a cosmic system within which the atoms themselves, which have become heavy through their interlacing, conglomerate toward the earth, the fine atoms forming the heavenly bodies, and so forth.

From this portrayal of the world formation the following emerges for the being of the things themselves: an appearance is what shows itself to us as the unity of a thing's form. In truth, each one is many, and many can never grow into an actual one, just as the actual one, the indivisible unity of the atom, can ever really become many. All of what is is a mixture of fullness and emptiness, which means, however, that emptiness—as that which holds things apart from one another—is the actual 'cause' of the formed unities that appear. For only what is held apart, a swarm of atoms in the void, can join itself together into the unity of a form. The process of this jointure itself obeys purely mechanical laws. The continuous agitation of the particles brings them into contact with one another. Insofar as they do not ricochet off of one another again (as the perception of 'solid' bodies teaches us—in contrast to the restless movement demonstrated by the perception of solar particles), the fact that these particles stay together on the basis of this contact makes a further assumption necessary: that the particles differentiate themselves according to shape and size. Thus they can interlink themselves firmly with one another. Small and smooth atoms will escape the entanglement of these concentrations the most easily; however, the cluster of tightly intertwined atoms will always hold the

J. Hammer-Jensen (*Archiv für Geschichte der Philosophie* XXIII, 1910) and Eva Sachs (*Philologischen Untersuchungen*, 24, 1917). See VS 54 A 1.

smooth atoms fast to themselves, and, most importantly, not all of the emptiness between the particles will ever be eliminated. The massive body is like the pile of letters at a print shop. The impression of 'solidity' is established only through the smallness of the atoms.[10]

And just as the appearance of the unity of things explains itself through these simplest assumptions of emptiness and atoms differentiated by size and shape, so all the qualities of these appearing things result from the form, situation, and position of these atoms, and all apparent changes of these qualities result from the simple rearrangement of these same characteristics. Thus, color, for instance, is established by the simple rearrangement of atoms and bodily weight by the sheer agglomeration of the atoms.

There is no doubt that this theory intends a consistent mechanical mode of explaining natural occurrence in the atomic realm. One can glean the basic laws of mechanics from these descriptions with no particular difficulty—the theories of collision and gravitation, for instance, the law of causality, the principles of the conservation of matter and energy, action and reaction, the law of entropy, and so on.[11] *But we will see that it is no accident that the principles of such a Democritan mechanics remain unformulated.* Furthermore, it is also indisputable that fruitful mechanical explanations have been associated with this universal theory of atomic mechanics by Democritus and along the entire line of the natural science of the time. Suggestive anecdotes and a plethora of very promising titles testify to Democritus' propensity for research into the mechanical causes of all appearances. He is supposed to have said that he would rather find one single causal proof for something than gain the throne of the Persian kingdom (VS Fragment 118). Thus he turns into a researcher precisely because he rejects the explanation that appearances are accidental. If only we are able to look keenly enough, we can always discover a compelling cause for any appearance.[12] The successful strength of the mechanical

10. See, esp., VS 55 A 37, 38.
11. This is consistently followed through *ad absurdum* in the work of L. Löwenheim, *Die Wissenschaft Demokrits und ihr Einfluß auf die moderne Naturwissenschaft*, Berlin 1914.
12. See Aristotle, *Physics* B 4.

concept of causality, taken together with a ruthless reduction of all qualitative factors to the true world of atomic forms, makes Democritan science a genuine model for the natural science of modernity—or so it would seem.

However, this conclusion must be examined. The idea that a Greek philosopher is supposed to have lived out in advance the ethos and methods of modern natural science, even more than this science itself, leaves us lacking an answer to the question of what this research and this knowledge drive meant to him within the whole of his philosophical worldview. For the judgment of history—a history that for two millennia has awarded victory to the opponents of this Atomism—can prove nothing here. Admittedly, it is no doubt correct to say that the bold conception of this atomic theory lacked the means of carrying itself out in the details of research: this overarching mechanistic interpretation was missing precise knowledge of the mechanics of colliding bodies, it completely lacked quantitative experimentation, but, above all, it lacked a mathematics that could have measured up to the abstractive heights of its basic assumptions. But the crucial thing is that it nevertheless claimed validity. And thus all of these observations—which from the standpoint of modern natural science signify just as many inner impossibilities for this atomic physics and reduce it to a kind of oddly prescient fantasy—all of them push the question concerning its basic philosophical motives into the foreground.

We will approach this question through a progressive series of observations:

1. By what means do the Atomists prove the existence of atoms? The intuition that guides them is that what genuinely is can never not be, which means, of course, that it persists unalterably. This means, however, that it must be something that remains unperturbed by the visible disintegration of all nature things. The line of reasoning that Aristotle cites[13] as the crucial grounds for the idea of the atom sounds 'mathematical'—or, more precisely: by appealing to the nature of the corporeal, it refutes the mathematical demand for a fundamentally unlimited divisibility posited by the idea of a continuum. Divisibility is based on the void; for otherwise it would entail the destruction of substance. Unlimited divisibility would therefore let everything

13. Aristotle, *On Generation and Corruption*, A 2, 315b ff.

corporeal pass away into the incorporeal, dimensionless, point-like void. The being of the corporeal, that is, would be nothing other than the void. In truth, however, the corporeal is a plenum, that in which there is no emptiness, the atom of indestructible form. The idea of the atom is thus an ontological postulate and proves to be an attempt to combine the thought of being in the Eleatic doctrine of unity with the demands of our experience of nature through the fact that it recognizes the true being of appearances in the multiplicity of invisible smaller unities.[14]

2. The indivisibility of the atoms is therefore an ontological/ physical demand, not a mathematical one. They are indivisible because they are 'solid,' that is, free of the void. Essentially, it is not their smallness that lets them be indivisible. They are not mathematical pseudo-points. They have various sizes; indeed, by itself, the theory could allow for atoms as big as the whole world—if only the experience of actual appearances did not exclude it.[15] It is a very controversial question whether a 'mathematical' Atomism (a construction of the continuum of empty space from extended 'points') corresponds to this 'physical' Atomism. The only testimony that could speak on behalf of this is the famous problem of sectioning a cone by parallel slices, which has even been interpreted as an anticipation of the principle of the infinitesimal.[16] But for Democritus it is expressly a 'physical' problem; that is, here too—as he no doubt did in the whole of his mathematics—Democritus may have adhered to the physical model and played out its true atomic structure against the intuitive demand of the continuum. Even 'authentic' knowledge, the knowledge of 'what is understood,' which Democritus opposed to the 'inauthentic' knowledge of the senses, was physical knowledge and not ideal mathematical knowledge.[17]

14. See VS 54 A, 8 and footnote 12.
15. See VS 55 A 47, 43; Aristotle *On Generation and Corruption* 326a 28.
16. VS 55 B, 155 and Diels' remarks.
17. In Democritus, therefore, it is essentially wrong to speak of an atomistic mathematics, but just as wrong to speak of an authentic mathematics of the continuum. Simplicius, in *Physics* 82, 1, has no worthwhile sources. The objection raised by Aristotle against Democritus regarding the conflict of his atomism with mathematics essentially confirms that Democritus did not recognize a genuine mathematics along with his true physics at all (see, for instance, VS Fragment 11 p!). Aristotle's

3. The Atomists declare the number of atoms to be unlimited because of the unlimited manifoldness of the appearances that need to be explained by them. This proposition allows us access to the basic ideological strengths of this interpretation of nature. The atoms are *innumerable*. Aristotle, of course, explains it this way: "In certain respects the Atomists, like the Pythagoreans, made everything into numbers" (VS 54 A 15), and, in fact, every existing thing is a multiplicity of atoms, thus it is a number. But neither is this number-being the being of things, nor are these numbers always quantifiable and familiar to us. Moreover, the interference or rearrangement of one single atom can decisively change the entire look of the atomic figure.[18] Thus genuine knowledge that gets behind sensory appearance certainly acknowledges that there are no accidents and that everything has its reasons; it just does not, however, acknowledge these reasons themselves. Its achievement, rather, is only that the observation of appearances facilitates the tireless drive of the real science of causality that lies within it, the idea that everything happens as it should, that everything, governed by the same mechanical necessity, happens 'by itself.' Admittedly, what we can know of nature is always only the rough connection of obvious causal connections, not the true mechanism of the atoms, the mechanism that presents the actual processes.[19]

4. Thus, by themselves, obeying the force of a movement within which they already are and always have been, the atoms

objection transfers Atomism to the problematic status of later noetic mathematics and approximates the doctrine of the 'indivisible line' of Plato and Xenocrates. Erich Frank gets it correct in *Platon und die sogenannten Pythagoreer* 1923, p. 54. See, above all, VS 55 B 11.

18. See VS 54 A 9.

19. No testimony proves that Democritus ever assumed a numerically determined mixture of atoms of various kinds—as we know Empedocles did. If, alongside Aristotle and prior to Empedocles, he is named as the first one to make reference to the essential definition of things, then the example of 'the warm' (*Metaphysics* 1076 B 20) proves what is meant by this. The appearance of heat is led back primarily to the same true essence, smooth and round fire-atoms, thus to differences in the form of the atoms, and not their number. Where relationships in the mixture of the variously formed atoms should explain an appearance—for instance, that of mixed colors—no precise numerical relationship is referred to. Thus, being a *sum* of atoms, the 'arithmetic' constitution of corporeal being provided no justification for an 'arithmetic.'

join themselves to the ephemeral unity of the bodily form. And just as the shapes of this world are constantly forming themselves from out of the atomic force, so other worlds are also constantly forming themselves according to the same laws. Admittedly, we know nothing at all about these worlds, and we can know nothing of them, but they are there, nevertheless. Nothing entitles us to think that our world, the world that we know, originated for a reason other than the senseless mechanism of atomic events. But wherever atoms amass themselves, this mechanism must lead to world formation. Obviously, such an interpretation of the world comes into the strictest tension with the natural experience of the world as a tangible, purposefully ordered cosmos.[20] As a rule, in this natural understanding of world the holding sway of necessity presents itself as the holding sway of contingency. Precisely because they alone are grounded on mechanical necessity, the shape of the cosmos and the cosmos of the shapes that fill up the world are nothing but a (happy) accident.[21] It was Attic philosophy that drew the philosophical consequences of this atomistic explanation of the world and triumphantly demonstrated its ideological [*weltanschauliche*] inversion, just as it demonstrated its factical incompleteness. The 'nature' that we know is not contingency producing itself out of blind inevitability but a meaningful living order (Plato, *Laws*, Book X).[22] And, furthermore:[23] the explanation of nature that is built upon the basic principles of Atomism never stops to see, for instance, the cause of the child in the father—that is, it never recognizes 'nature' as operative in this ordering of the event of propagation itself. Human propagation would originate by itself ('automatically'), the Atomists explained, and only from the more remote event of world formation, the event in which the order of the heavens comes into being, and from the

---

20. See Plato's characteristic word play in the *Timaeus* (55 c–d), where Plato declares the doctrine of 'boundlessly' many worlds to be a 'boundless' speculation (*apeiros*).

21. For this inner connection of mechanism, purposefulness, and contingency, see, above all, Kant (for instance, *Critique of Judgment*, §61).

22. Cf. the phrases, *physis kai tuchê*, in *Protagoras* 323 c, *Laws* 889 a 5, and similarly: *kata tuchên ex anankês*, in *Laws* 889 c 1, in contrast to Plato's *psychê... diapherontôs physei*, in the *Laws*, 892 c.

23. See Aristotle, *Physics* B 4 = VS 55 A 69.

processes of inanimate nature. It was the great accomplishment of Aristotelian philosophy of nature to have shown the inner imperfection of this Atomistic interpretation of nature and to have found its ontological expression in the proximity of the 'by itself' and contingency.

Within the atomistic idea of nature there lies a distortion of the natural picture of the world oriented toward the forms of things and living beings and, along with this distortion, a *depletion of meaning from all events*.[24] Necessity, which dominates everything and according to which everything occurs by itself, operates as the meaningless cause of a nevertheless meaningful end result[25]: the natural order. But, then, it is certainly not an originary force of nature. Whatever originates and occurs with regularity is not the work of contingency. That which happens against the rule and the expected effect is contingent. Thus the concept of the 'by itself'—in Democritus the exclusive expression of inescapable necessity before the fundamental lawfulness of the natural order—gains the character of an absolute cause, the character, that is, of that which leads blindly to a consequence that, otherwise, the fundamental laws of nature or conscious purpose are in the habit of producing. This may not be a meaningful definition for an investigation of nature based on a consistently mechanical methodology, but it is the logical extension of an atomistic interpretation of nature that has never really relinquished its orientation toward the experienced order of the cosmos.

5. The juncture at which the real underlying world of the atoms and the world of the natural experience come together lies in sense perception. The reality of the appearance of unitary forms and qualitative differences substantiates itself, as does the supposition of atoms, in the atomistic interpretation of sensory perception. Here we find the doctrine of primary and secondary qualities that is so crucial for modern philosophy and its attitude toward natural science. The basic assumption of the absolute reality of atoms and their movement through the void allows the content of sensory perception to be considered only as appearance. But, at the same time, this appearance is what is true as it shows itself. The subjectivity of the sensations has its

24. [*eine Sinnentleerung alles Geschehens*]
25. [*die sinnlose Ursache einer dennoch sinnhaften Endwirkung*]

true ground in the true being of reality, the atoms. In the innumerable throng of atoms that composes a corporeal appearance, all of the atomic forms and figurations are really found in that which leads to the changing and subjectively various sensations. The same wine tastes sweet to one person and dry to another because the one person is actually receptive to and pervious to this atomic form and the other person to that one. Genuine perception [*echte Erkenntnis*], therefore, always allows us to assume the sole reality of the atoms and the void in all apparent sense data.

Obviously, we do determine the size, shape, and location of atoms in that we analogically translate the mechanical properties of the things known from our sense experience back to the atoms. And any real investigation of causes in the field of natural science happens completely within the coarser conspicuousness of the shapes of things as they appear. Democritus, therefore, can supplement his critical delimitation of the truth of sense perception by counterposing the criticism of the senses to the action of the understanding: "Miserable understanding, you take your evidence from us and want to defeat us with it? Your triumph is your downfall."[26] The skepticism of late antiquity was therefore not all that mistaken when, in phrases like, "that we cannot recognize how each thing in truth is constituted,"[27] it found the senses and the understanding bewildered in the same way. And we comprehend from the skeptical resignation of this Democritan atomic science that Aristotle commits no mere folly when, over against the atomistic interpretation of the qualitative changes in nature, he refers at one point to sensory experience, which sees a whole changing itself as a whole.[28] For, of course, the processes of the transposition of atoms, by means of which Democritus explains changes, are supposed to be precisely invisible. Aristotle is nevertheless quite right: the interpretive description of the processes of nature themselves, as we initially experience them with our senses, imposes upon us different ways of apprehending events in their entirety. In contrast to the assumption of the atoms and their summative arithmetic figuration, these modes of apprehension constitute the true

26. VS 55 B 125.
27. VS 55 B 10; see Fragments 6–9.
28. Aristotle, *On Generation and Corruption*, A 9 327a, 15 ff.

metaphysics of nature. For it is not isolated particles, indifferent to one another, joining together or reordering themselves, that are the primary being of reality but rather forms [*Gestalten*]. And these forms do not just spring out of the dice shaker of contingency. They—and not the *atomic* 'Ur-forms'[29]—constitute the controlling unity of the processes that we want to explain.

6. From the perspective of modern mechanical natural science—which, with its methodical consciousness, restricts the concept of nature to the *scibile*[30] in the mathematical sense of the word and therefore knows that it pays for each advance toward precise knowledge with the increasing impoverishment of every advance it makes toward the nature of the object of its knowledge—Democritus admittedly attains the honorary rank of an early precursor, and from the perspective of Aristotle's final unitary worldview the intuition appears as a paralyzing dogmatism. On the other hand, whoever pays attention to the ideological forces that are operative in various places recognizes in Aristotle's vision of the world the magnificent attempt, through a reformulation of the most ancient truth, to banish the explanation that, from Democritus on, led to the most extreme dissolution of all combinatory and form-developing forces. A glimpse into the ethical fragments of Democritus (which, admittedly, we must liberate from much later embellishment) would confirm that we have correctly combined the ideological foundations of his prodigious research energy with the basic idea of his atomic theory. The encompassing horizon of Greek common sense, as Plato and Aristotle sought to reproduce it in a later time, is no longer the sustaining certainty of this icy intellect.

7. The counterforce that works itself out in Aristotle's view of the world is of *Platonic origin*. It is not without reason that we have characterized the whole literary work of Plato as one single great dialogue with Democritus, and the ancient anecdote that Plato wanted to burn the Democritan writings and that he only refrained from doing it because the texts were already in too many hands is not without deeper symbolic value. But was not Plato himself—right alongside Democritus and of no less historical effect than him—the creator of an atomistic theory of matter and elements? Does his inimitable greatness not lie

29. [*die* atomaren '*Urgestalten*']
30. [Latin for "knowable."]

precisely in the fact that he himself embraced this truth of modernity? In fact, the most modern natural science came to recognize basic anticipations of its own discoveries in Plato no less than in Democritus.[31]

It would be going too far to show in detail which deep instincts the exploration of ancient natural philosophy—as measured against the standard of natural science—followed when, in spite of this, it saw the true ancient precursor of natural science not in Plato but rather in Democritus. The transformation that the Democritan idea of the atom undergoes in the *mythos* of the *Timaeus* may indicate what the mechanical natural science of modernity admits about itself when it feels more deeply bound to Democritan Atomism than to Platonic. Plato's ultimate elementary unities, out of which he thinks the material of the world is constituted—and only this material, not the world-order itself!—are triangles. The triangle, however, is the simplest figure into which three-dimensional mathematical figures are divisible. The assumption of the indivisibility of ultimate atomic triangles is thus based on an *eidetic* indivisibility. For indivisibility is the essence of the triangle in the sense that no simpler *figure* results from it through further division. Plato's atoms are not ultimate realities withstanding the disintegration of apparent forms, the destruction of all formal unities; they are the primordial forms of the corporeal itself.[32] And they are not accidental figures that originate by joining together, but regular 'Platonic bodies.' The atomic triangles are not the final reality of a possible fragmentation of corporeality but the original building blocks of that which is well-ordered. They accomplish not a dissolution of all visible forms but rather the intuitive subdivision of the system of laws for that which is extended. This is why there is no void in the Platonic world of atoms. The mechanics of the atomic structure of matter have the character of a mathematical synthesis and not that of an anomalous inevitable event. In this radical transformation of the Democritan concept of the atom, we can fathom the effective energy in Plato that forces the explanation of Greek natural science once again under the fundamental law

---

31. Eva Sachs has propounded this position (*Philologischen Untersuchungen* 24, 1917) esp. page 221 f. See Kurt Hildebrandt, *Platon* (1933), p. 380 f.

32. [*die Urformen des Körperlichen selbst*]

of the Hellenic interpretation of existence. What is supposed to explain the true nature of reality for Democritus—the blind necessity of the inextricable atomic event—finds its limited authority in a double transformation in the mythic world creation of the *Timaeus*. That the world is, is an act of construction according to a divine mathematics. That there are in this world anomalous and imperfect things, that earthly events lack the pure perfection of the cosmic structure—this is the power of the blind force of the materiality that forms itself out of atoms. But even this atomistic formation of material reveals a mathematical preformation. The law of form and number still holds sway, even in the indiscernible. This mathematics of what is material is no more the result of a measuring and calculating analysis than is the mathematics that thoroughly orders the visible proportions of worldly bodies. It adapts itself to the basic plan according which the world is described. And if human existence has its definitive place in this plan, then, at the same time, the law of the world establishes the law of the human reality of civil community. This plan turns into an order that counters all the dissolving powers of the exhausted state spirit with the resistance of a new cosmic dignity. Thus our insights into the philosophical motives of ancient atomism confirm themselves in the contrasting image of this mythical founding of world and state.

It would require a separate presentation to show how, on the basis of this Platonic idea of the world, Aristotle became a critic of not just Democritan but Platonic atomism as well. We would recognize that this criticism of Plato's perception of nature, decisive for two thousand years, has remained steadfast, but not its civil passion, which meant binding the effective forces of antagonistic dangers to it instead of eliminating them.

When later historical research misapplied the self-certainty of the modern idea of science, looking past the Platonic-Aristotelian ideas of nature to see the precursor of modern natural science in Democritus, it did not just commit a mistake of historical knowledge: in the unquestioned validity of the standard of modern natural science a renunciation of philosophy in the higher sense revealed itself.

4

Plato and Presocratic Cosmology

"The tradition of Socrates is constituted in such a way that it is beyond all hope that the historian could reach a reliable conclusion from it": With this observation, Helmut Kuhn opens his 1934 afterword justifying his portrayal of Socrates;[1] he then refers to the concept of primordial history developed by Franz Overbeck in order to establish that he seeks not to reconstruct the historical Socrates from the disparate accounts of a variegated tradition, but rather to experience Socrates in his effect on Plato and the origin of Western metaphysics, and thus to encounter Socrates not at all in his historiographical contingency but in his historical reality. As I have tried to show elsewhere,[2] what happened in the transformation of the task of knowledge in the unique case of Socrates can be justified in its general and principle meaning. It is quite certain, however, that such historical realities, realities that fall into the category of 'beginning,' gain their determination only from the result and the end. Kuhn's above-mentioned statement, then, can be applied without any modification especially to the beginning of Western philosophy in the

1. Helmut Kuhn, *Sokrates*, Munich 1960, p. 129. My review of [the 1934 edition of] this book [Die Runde, Berlin] shows how much the basic methodological ideas of Kuhn's book had already been influencing me for decades. (*Deutsche Literaturzeitung* 57, 1936, pp. 96–100; reprinted in GW 5, pp. 322–326.)
2. *Wahrheit und Methode*, Tübingen, 1960 (= GW 1), especially pp. 284 ff.

early Greeks. What these earliest thinkers were (thinkers whom we know by the names of Thales, Anaximander and Anaximenes) cannot be unambiguously reconstructed either from the older or the more recent tradition—thus the picture of the scholarship and its progress is essentially one in which a supposed certainty crumbles repeatedly and the degree of uncertainty grows. And even though we possess (albeit from a slightly later time) a considerable portion of Parmenides' didactic poem and a series of unambiguously original statements from Heraclitus, for all that, these 'founts' themselves flow in a disturbing darkness of uncertainty, as does, for instance, the Pythagoras problem or the Orphic problem with which every well-educated person is familiar. And, as this darkness slowly lightens in the fifth century, Empedocles, Anaxagoras, and Democritus obtain a reliable outline for us, so that with regard to the whole of the Presocratic tradition we are still undoubtedly in the same situation that holds for the problem of Socrates: Plato, with his dialogues, and Aristotle, with his lecture notes (the two figures who begin the literary tradition of Greek philosophy for us), have so saturated and shaped the entire Presocratic tradition that is accessible to us that we, at the very height of historical critique and with all of its tools, hardly have a viewpoint from which to discern anything with certainty other than the picture of this history impressed upon us by Plato and, above all, by Aristotle. From this point on, whatever there is of a completely uninfluenced tradition can hardly be isolated—perhaps at best we could mention here the large excerpt from Parmenides' didactic poem, yet even this transcription, which was acquired faithfully by Simplicius, is a choice, and, like every choice, it is influenced and it has influence.

Nevertheless, it would be misguided—even here—to believe that we need to content ourselves with this and to believe that no other avenue of investigation stands more open to us. Even here, by going back to infer the effect that they had on their progenitors, that is, from the way that Plato and Aristotle explicitly or implicitly mirror the Presocratic tradition, there exists the possibility of learning something about what these first thinkers were. There is, of course, an initial critical insight that cannot be circumvented: namely, that we must not only reject the belief in the *interpretatio aristotelica* (for which Theophrastus and the doxographers laid the ground), but that, just as vehemently, we must also reject the one *interpretatio* that—in spite of all the

anti-Hegelianism of the historical school—governs the collected
historical and philological thought of the moderns, which I like
to call the *interpretatio hegeliana*. This interpretation's self-
evident presupposition is certainly not, as it is in Hegel, the
total comprehensibility of history from the perspective if its inner
'logic'—but this much is also certain about this presupposition: that the individual thinkers and their teachers refer to one
another, 'surpass,' criticize, and struggle with one another, in such
a way that the dialogue of the tradition is ordered by a logically
intelligible context.

This may be generally true: the above presupposition may not
be in order where a tradition can generally be acquired only
from the testimony of those who came later, as in the case of the
Presocratics. We do not know, for example, if Parmenides was
even acquainted with Heraclitus; we do not know what the
Milesian 'school' looked like, whether the received diadoche[3]
is anything more than a later concoction. We do not know who
Pythagoras really was. And, above all, the Platonic ordering
hardly observes the temporal succession of the earlier thinkers
any more than the Aristotelian one does, and it arranges them
according to their 'systematic' viewpoints. Given the disposi-
tion of this tradition, then, it would mean overestimating what
it is possible to know if we were to try to reconstruct a historical
succession and if we were to attempt to differentiate the individual thinkers and their doctrines and to derive them from one
another, as has generally been the case. It seems to me that the
reverse task has been posed, and right now the latest research in
this field confirms it: only the common motives and problems that
unite them all promise an entry into these beginnings that touches
upon their reality.

The way that Plato sees his 'predecessors' fulfills this task best
of all. For, with the lone exception of the Eleatics, he saw them
all as a unit and christened them with a single name—the
'Heracliteans.'[4] It is obvious that this way of conceiving the tradition is an antithetical development, that its real motive is the
positive appropriation of the Eleatic thought of being through the
doctrine of the ideas. Thus the effective history of Eleatic thought

---

3. [Succession; Gadamer is referring here to the generally accepted
sequence of Thales, Anaximander, Anaximenes, Heraclitus, Parmenides.]
4. *Theaetetus* 179 d–e.

will always be an essential entryway into the Eleatic doctrine, and Plato stands at the cusp of it.[5]

Working against this, on the other hand, is the subject matter of the Ionians, who blend in with Heraclitus and those who came later precisely because of the Eleatic antithesis into which Plato pushes them. Conversely, if we now wanted to lean on Aristotle for our view of the Ionians (the man who relegated Eleatic philosophy to the fringe because of his disagreement about *kinesis* and regarded Ionian 'philosophy of nature' positively), we would overlook how much anti-Pythagoreanism and anti-Platonism there is in the pre-history of Aristotle's 'metaphysics' (which is essentially a physics). As Helmut Kuhn correctly worked out in his book on Socrates, it really is the case that, in his effect on Plato, Socrates represents the origin of metaphysics, even if in Plato metaphysics is the same thing as 'physics.' But precisely what makes Plato an incomparable witness to the beginnings of philosophy is that he had achieved his own doctrine in the Socratic renunciation of this older tradition, or better: *in his conscious response to this tradition.* To understand his philosophy as an answer means to arrive at the question that was raised with the early beginnings of Greek philosophy. There is no more concise, no more immediate hermeneutic possibility than the one that opens itself here: the question here is not one of the plausibility of witnesses, or of conscious interpretations and depictions, but rather the peculiar possibilities of Platonic thinking. What were the Presocratics—more particularly, what were the Ionians—if Plato could situate them over against his Socrates in this way?

If we start here, then the *Timaeus* steps into the spotlight. Its multi-layered whole (which looks only as far back as its own task demands) expresses something more immediate about the Presocratics than those most highly suggestive retrospectives on the earlier philosophers that we find in the *Phaedo*, the *Theaetetus*, or the *Sophist* and whose particulars we certainly should not neglect.[6]

5. See my work, "Zur Vorgeschichte der Metaphysik", in *Anteile: Martin Heidegger zum 60. Geburtstag*, Frankfurt am Main, 1950, pp. 51–79 (= GW 6, pp. 9–29).

6. *Phaedo* 96 a ff.; *Theaetetus* 152 d ff., 180 c ff.; *Sophist* 242 c ff.

In its proper existence and essence,[7] the *Timaeus* is perhaps not just a great dialogue with Democritus (as many have interpreted it),[8] but, taken on its own terms, it is, rather, a historical point of entry into earlier thinking as a whole. As we know, insofar as he refers to the Platonic dialogical works in his *Metaphysics*, Aristotle has the *Timaeus* chiefly in mind. And in all of his critiques of Plato we find the idea that Plato explained the participation of phenomena in the Ideas by means of 'empty metaphors'—empty metaphors, that is, drawn from the domain of *technê* for something which is not grounded in *technê*; yet, in his doctrine of the four causes, Aristotle himself follows the model of *technê* in order to grasp conceptually what a *physei on* is. The *Timaeus* is certainly not a 'Platonic *Physics*,' to which the Aristotelian *Physics* corresponds and follows; for the *Timaeus* is a *mythos*, a story, that does not demand the credibility and truth of a *logos*. But, like all Platonic *mythoi*, these are not fables foreign to the *logos*, foreign to knowledge, but rather an imaginative projection from out of what is known within the *logos*. Since the intelligible being of the *eidos* is supposed to determine what is visible outside the domain of the producible, Plato tries to say what the *eidos* is by way of production.

Indeed it appears to have been a controversial question among the Platonists whether the *fabricatio mundi* that the *Timaeus* recounts actually meant that the world came into being or whether, 'because of its didacticism,' it is to be interpreted as a mathematical construct.[9] Aristotle himself alludes to this, and Proclus reports on the details. What suggests again and again that we are not to understand the production of the world literally is the *Timaeus*' doctrine that a world-order structured in this way will be eternal. The Aristotelian argument against anything having become eternal is so close to and agrees so compellingly with Plato himself that we find ourselves directed toward the mythical character of the *Timaeus* narrative.

---

7. [*Dasein und Sosein*, literally, "there-being and thus-being."]

8. See E. Frank, *Plato und die sogenannten Pythagoreer*, p. 118 ff.

9. Cf. Plutarch, *Moralia, De fato*, 568 c. The significance of this reliable tradition lies in the fact that, in passages like the *Sophist* 243 a–b, the 'de-mythologizers' were in no way disconcerted. Thus, they also did not take this seriously!

Obviously, what is specifically mythical in this bold and unprecedented story is the idea that this world was made—and not that it came into being. It is not just the Aristotelian polemic that clearly presupposed that notions of having come into being were prevalent among the ancients; this also appears, for instance, in the critical/ironical depictions of the genealogical fairy tales that we find in the *Sophist*.[10] There can be no doubt, therefore, that our account of the 'cosmogonical' doctrine of the Ionians, especially that of Anaximander, contains something that is correct. Nevertheless, a glance at the *Timaeus* for the meaning of these cosomogonies is quite informative. In fact, they clearly culminate in the derivation of an existing cosmic order that holds itself in a spontaneous balance in exactly the same way that the artful production of the world order by the Demiurges of the *Timaeus* depicts the emergent order as a persistent integrated formation of mathematical harmonies in a reality that is not free of oppositions. There can be no doubt: the cosmogony of early thought was intended for the sake of cosmology.

We can now definitely say that all cosmogony is recounted for the sake of cosmology. It is of the essence of the matter that the story told about the world is the story of what exists now—in all its imposing order and regularity. Even the religious cosmogonies—the Orphic, the Babylonian, the Egyptian—have this connotation. It therefore makes a crucial difference whether a cosmogonical tale tells us much about its wonders by starting from an egg, or from *Eros*, or from Night—intuitive models for the wonder of becoming—or whether such tales, completely and thoroughly dominated and determined by the intuition of a prefect end, explain the becoming of this world by means of the same forces and processes that visibly control and constitute them. Uvo Hölscher, who delved into the influence of the oriental myths,[11] rightly raises the point that Hesiod, after all, tells us nothing intuitive about the primordial conditions—very much in contrast to the Eastern origin stories: "The poets occupied themselves, not with how the world originated, but rather with how it is arranged" (401).

10. *Sophist* 242 c ff.
11. *Hermes* 81 (1953), p. 257 ff., 385 ff.; reprinted in Uvo Hölscher, *Anfängliche Fragen. Studien zur frühen griechischen Philosophie*. Göttingen 1968.

I mean that, in a sharper analysis of its meaning, the old question of whether cosmology or cosmogony stands at the beginning of Greek philosophizing cancels itself out, and it is precisely the *Timaeus* that shows the inappropriateness of this line of questioning. For example: in the accounts of Anaximander we repeatedly run into a contradiction that posits the idea of the *apeiron*, on the one hand, as that of a 'beginning' out of which whatever is opposed excludes itself and, on the other hand, as the grand balanced order in which oppositions are controlled and connected (so that, even with the best intentions, we cannot find fault with Aristotle when he asks why the world needed to be one of an endless supply of created worlds if one that is so well balanced in its oppositions—or even a succession of such worlds that displace one another—can be formed from one and the same mass); thus it seems to me that this contradiction, which to this day leaves the interpretation defenseless, cannot be seen as much different, logically speaking, from the 'created eternity' depicted in the *Timaeus*. It is certainly not accidental that in Anaximander, whose well ordered constitution stands confidently in the center of his doctrine, the question of the dissolution of the world remains obscure. Was there such a dissolution at all—or is it like in the *Timaeus*? And must we not, then, look upon the 'many worlds' tradition differently?

Inspired by the *Timaeus* once again, must we not test the whole question anew? But, of course, this is why the reliably reported doctrine of the multiplicity of 'worlds' is generally thought to refer to temporal succession in such a way that it gives rise to fatal contradictions; because they considered co-existence too monstrous a thing, it was contemplated only in the extreme atomism of the late fifth century, which had confidence in the transgression of all possible experiences and intuitions.[12]

But, let us test this doctrine against the account in the *Timaeus*.[13] There the doctrine of the many or even the innumerably many *(apeiroi) kosmoi* or *ouranoi* encounters an explicit

12. G. S. Kirk, in: Kirk and Raven, *The Presocratic Philosophers*, Cambridge, 1957, p. 121 ff. and Charles Kahn, *Anaximander and the Origins of Greek Cosmology*, 1960, p. 46 ff. Yet, see Julia Kerschensteiner, *Kosmos*, 1962, who flawlessly defends the doxographical tradition (p. 38 ff.).
13. *Timaeus* 31 a f.

repudiation and indeed prepares for these difficulties with an argument. Evidently, the Platonic schema of replicating according to a model (*kata to paradeigma dedêmiourgêmenos*, 31 a 2) has to demonstrate the 'uniqueness' of the world, though not quite as easily as Aristotle does; Aristotle could rely on the idea of all matter being used up, while Plato must first prove the singularity of this world of ours in another way (*Timaeus*, 33 a). His argument from replicating according to the pattern of the most perfect of all, the living being that encompasses all living things (*panteches zôon*, 31 b 1), is completely problematic. There is still no mention of matter here. Plato wants, rather, to demonstrate the uniqueness of our world from pure ideas, that is, from essential relations. The uniqueness in the model, the idea of a living being that encompasses all living beings, logically derives from the idea of the model in the familiar way,[14] that is, that a second model would make necessary the regress to a One that encompasses both. This may be clear. But it is all the more complicated now that the copy is supposed to be solely that which is one as well. Yet it belongs precisely to the essential structure of the copy and of the imitation that many imitations of a model are possible. What is a resemblance *kata tên monôsin*[15] (b 2) really supposed to mean?

Or, better yet: if the production of the visible world in view of the one model is supposed to make the question of many worlds answerable, must we not conclude from this that the question did not seem answerable to Plato without his mythical story of the demiurges? And, even though the their names are nowhere mentioned by him, should it not really be just Leucippus and Democritus who are intended here? What is it, then, that produces the *technê*-model employed for this argument? Evidently, it is this: that the idea of the whole—that which is encompassed as the unity that everything is—is first thought in *anticipation* of the whole. This agrees completely with the mode of argumentation in the *Phaedo*, where the introduction of a certain hypothesis of the *eidos* is demonstrated in the example of the two—I underscore *the* two—which 'originates' neither from joining together nor from separation but rather is the unity of the two.

14. [An anticipation of Aristotle's so-called third man argument.]
15. ['according to its uniqueness or oneness']

110 *The Beginning of Knowledge*

If, as Heribert Boeder[16] plausibly states, it is correct to say that the early Ionians called the whole into which they inquired *ta panta*, then this nomenclature already expresses an insufficient understanding of unity, an understanding that was tied to the idea of that which encompasses everything. It is evident that the idea of the *apeiron* as the limitless expansion of being—an expansion that never comes to an end—precisely leaves the idea of the one, the whole, unexpressed (and, certainly, anyone who does not seek to defend a preconceived thesis will probably understand the Anaximandrian phrase in this spatial sense).

Thus, the testimony of the *Timaeus* seems to betray a fundamental deficiency among the *physikoi* from outset (admittedly, Xenophanes and Parmenides do not belong to this list, but the fact that Plato considers the Eleatics the precursors of his doctrine of ideas does apply to them), and thus it seems to testify indirectly to the intuition followed by the first Ionians: the idea of the 'from itself' that characterizes the origination and continued existence of our world. This may not have a radical meaning approaching that of the atomistic cosmogony. But does not the idea of the limitless as the *archê*, the idea of a condition of being that exists as an inexhaustible supply in advance of all world-becoming, suggest the idea of many worlds that 'exclude themselves' from out of this *archê*, and that, even if they do this one after another, they do it in such a way that each one, as a self-contained structure, would have permanence and so exist next to the others? Would this really be impossible? Is this not, in fact, necessary if we want to think the doctrine of the limitless together with the doctrine of the balance of opposites at all? Was Anaximander not also hazarding an unprecedented and audacious idea when, instead of the divinity of the Homeric or Hesiodic gods, he thought the 'divinity' of limitless being?

In regard to this, a central motif of earlier thought once again dating from the time of Plato now appears: the attempt to explain the situation of the Earth at the center of the universe without the help of the mythological figure of Atlas. This emerges in Plato as he distances himself critically from the earlier thinkers who adopt a 'new' Atlas in the form of air turbulence or a cushion of air upon which to situate the earth and as he himself,

16. 12 Heribert Boeder, *Grund und Gegenwart als Frageziel der frühgriechischen Philosophie*, The Hague, 1962, p. 23 f.

completely avoiding all of this, wants to arrive at his explanation entirely from the idea of the good: *Phaedo* 99 c. How he imagines this, however, is expressed most clearly by the *mythos* of the *Phaedo* (108e): the *homoiotês*[17] of the heavens, their *isorropia*,[18] would suffice to keep the earth in the middle without tilting. Admittedly, this is a semi-mythical description once again, resonating with more of a Pythagorean tone of ideal geometrical symmetry than a dynamic balancing relationship. But this is especially instructive. For later in Aristotle we read something similar that surely refers to Anaximander: "Because of *homoiotês*, that which has its seat in the middle will remain in its place" (VS A 26). Of course (as, amazingly enough, Charles Kahn suggests[19]), we can trace this Aristotle citation back—though with difficulty—to the authority of at least Hippolytus, who argues in an entirely geometrical way. Ultimately, however, such a 'geometrical teleology' probably only fits a spherical conception of the earth like we find in the *Phaedo*. There, however, we have the most unambiguous testimony for Anaximander ascribing to the earth the shape of a truncated column, just as Hippolytus himself reports in the doxography (VS A 25). It can only be one or the other!

Instead, we will have to seek another originary meaning in the *homoiosis* thesis besides the geometrical one that Aristotle wanted to find in Anaximander. But this could only have been an idea of balance like the kind Plato criticized as being the invention of a new Atlas—perhaps a cushion of air, like in Anaximander (A 20). In point of fact, with the exception of Anaximander's flat, truncated column, I now believe this to have been an original motif of Ionian cosmology, a further demonstration of which can be seen in Thales. The only thing we know for certain about Thales is that, among other things, he also altered his doctrine of water so that the earth would float on the water like a piece of wood. We can trust this report as authentic because Aristotle criticizes it: as if we were not then left with the same problem of how the water that carries the earth (*ochountos!*[20]) would keep from

17. ['homogeneity'; 'being of similar substance']
18. ['equipoise']
19. Kahn, *Anaximander and the Origins of Greek Cosmology*, Hackett 1985 (originally published in 1960) p. 76 ff.
20. ['carrying']

sinking out of its own place. Apparently, what is shown to us here is that this particular *homoiotês* is based upon Aristotle's separation of the Ionians from the theologians; it is an observation referring to Thales as if it had referred to a 'proof': wood floats on the water in such a way that the water always drives it, as it were, toward the surface. What we call 'water displacement' was apparently thought of as an amazing natural phenomenon of balancing: that is, not the *homoiotês* of similar geometrical spaces, but probably—as the *Phaedo* actually says, as well—*isorropia*, an *antereisis*,[21] as it is called in the doxography of Anaximenes, Anaxagoras, and Democritus (A 20). Anaximenes, it seems, needed a no-less-ingenious *apodeixis* for his air cushion: the water in a water clock. Thus behind the critique and behind Plato's Pythagorean theology we grasp something of a universal cosmological motif for the Ionians. In his own mythical argument from symmetry, Plato still lets something of the ancients shine through when he speaks of *isorropia*. In truth, his own theological/eidetic 'cosmology' demands a purely geometrical argument: instead of a new Atlas, the self-containment of the whole was to be thought.

As the examples we have followed through show, the underlying methodological idea that guides us is the fact that the Platonic answer made the reconstruction of the question posed by Presocratic thinking possible, the fact that the adequate conceptuality that determines all of our testimony from Aristotle on was not yet available to them. From the same methodological viewpoint, what Plato carries out regarding the concept of the *psychê* in explicit counterpoint to the Presocratic tradition is also highly suggestive. The graduated path of argumentation that the Platonic *Phaedo* carries out culminates in the proof of immortality based on the *eidos* of life. It is the general insight into eidetic classes that parallels the incompatibility of the *psychê* and death with the incompatibility of heat and snow. A remarkable argument. To be sure, the order of being to which the soul belonged was developed from the essence of mathematical being; but, in the end, 'soul' refers to that which all the ancients also sought without really being able to think it: namely, the 'nature' of things. Indeed, this is what Socrates is depicting in the well-known expectation and disappointment that the writings of

21. ['thrusting against'; 'resistance']

Anaxagoras caused him. The idea of the good already becomes visible here as that which determines all true knowing of the ultimate end. Without this idea of the good—and this also means without the soul—the idea of *physis* cannot be thought. This is what secures for the *psychê* its central position in Platonic thinking. The idea of the good, especially as it is presented in the tenth book of the *Laws,* is the real essence of nature. Nature cannot be called the blind necessity or coming together of things, but rather the very condition of having been directed toward the good: *psychê* and *technê* denote the same thing (892 b 7). In this kind of honing down one will certainly recognize a counterpoint to the atomistic concept of nature in Leucippus and Democritus. But here, once again, just like the idea of the 'from itself,' the extreme sharpening of the idea of nature is an indirect, historically effected testimony for what the ancients intended without being able to truly think it: the order, constancy, and regularity of the whole of being. The *technê* model introduced by Plato makes this visible.

For that matter, however, there is a second model. The confrontation with the universal doctrine of motion presented in the *Theaetetus* is definitely not direct testimony for the ancient thought of the so-called Heracliteans. Rather this universal doctrine of motion is constructed from out of the Platonic concept of *eidos* and the concept of the soul given along with it. Plato pushes the more ancient thinking toward a radical conclusion that was the last thing on his mind. This is reflected perhaps most clearly—and we owe this insight mainly to Hermann Langerbeck[22]—in the way that the soul becomes distinguished from the senses, which, for their part, belong to the whole of the motion that they perceive. The soul knows by the means of this same whole; but this means that the soul is differentiated from it and opened into the only dimension of being in which there are truly existing beings. Here is where the concepts of *nous* and *noêsis* first obtained their specific articulation. At this point he means the knowing of true beings, the knowing that removes itself from that which is grasped in *aisthesis*, that which does not really exist but rather is always other than what really is. We can

22. Hermann Langerbeck, "*Doxis Epirusmie.* Studien zu Demokrits Ethik un Erkenntnislehre" in *Neue philologische Untersuchungen*, 10 (1934).

conclude from this (and this is certainly one of the most important insights of all that we have obtained from Plato about the Presocratics) that, in the Platonic sense, there was just as little an essential opposition between *aisthesis* and *noêsis* as there was an unambiguous concept of the *psychê*. This is no less important for Parmenides' doctrine of being than it is for the connection between soul and fire that appears in Heraclitus.[23]

The so-called Eleatic dialogues, however, play a very special role in our guiding methodological ideas. The *Sophist* grants the figures from Elea a superior position, just like the *Parmenides* does, but it is not so much that they play the Eleatic concept of being off against a universal Heracliteanism but rather that the Eleatics go beyond themselves. It is the new dimension of the *logos*—the Socratic/Platonic dimension—that is opened up by Eleatic means. But this necessitates a reformulating of the Eleatic doctrine, which, in turn, allows us to draw conclusions about the original doctrine.

First of all, we might establish that the confrontation with Parmenides' doctrine of being that runs through all the Platonic dialogues shifts the emphasis from *on* to *hen*. But in this way the Eleatic rejection of the many transforms itself into the dialectical assimilation of the many within the very concepts of being and the one. For the one is always the one of the many. With this, however, the essence of *logos* is for the first time correctly visible: for it is the essence of the *logos* to be the one in such a way that it does not simply posit what it has said and what has posited, but rather it expresses something, and it thereby turns into the many and stands apart from the many and yet is intended as one.

This should be just how it is with the concept of the whole. Like the concept of the one, this is also a concept that is implicit in the Parmenidean doctrine, and, as such, its significance still has yet to be unfolded. It is the Platonic dialectic that first accomplished this unfolding; that is, it discloses the essential inner dialectic that binds the concept of the whole with the concept of the part.[24] The argument in the *Sophist* that the concept of the

23. See my later work on Heraclitus in GW 7 and above.
24. *Sophist* 244 d ff. The aporia put forward by Aristotle (*Physics* A 2, 185 b 11–16) should therefore also be seen as Platonic–pointing back to the oral doctrine? See, esp., *Philebus* 14 d–e.

whole disintegrates dialectically—just as the concept of the one does—negatively mirrors how the single whole of Parmenidean being still maintains itself in the intuition and sheds no real light upon the entire dimension of *onoma* and *logos* and their dialectical implications.

How little the dimension of *logos* disclosed by this was conscious of its heterogeneity with respect to previous thinking is shown very clearly in the exposition of the *Sophist*. The conjoined concepts upon which everything is based, the concepts that constitute the *logos* as *logos* (being and non-being, sameness and difference), the concepts whose involvement with one another the *logos* alone makes at all possible, stand alongside two other supremely generic concepts that are of a completely different kind and origin: motion and stillness. Certainly they, too, came to bear on the analysis of the structure of the *logos* insofar as only an unchangeable motionless object can be an object of knowledge; and knowledge, for its part, is not possible without unfolding that which is itself different in being, that is, without change or movement occurring. As tiresome as it was for Plato to construct the Heraclitean/Eleatic opposition in this way so as to formalize the structural moments of the *logos*, it is just as instructive for us to the extent that, like the phenomenon of the *logos*, it lets us deduce from it the knowledge that in the whole of ancient thought the soul was still undifferentiated from beings, that is, from that which constituted being as the known. But this means that the opposition of *physis* and *psychê* and with it the concept of *physis*, like that of the *psychê*, is first to be obtained from the Platonic question frame.

We now direct our attention toward the explicit discussion of ancient thinking undertaken by the stranger in Plato's *Sophist* and toward the historical picture of the Presocratics that becomes comprehensible at that point; in this way we will make two astonishing observations. The first one is that here is where we first find the treatment of the history of philosophy that was dominated by Aristotle and the Peripatetics. In the *Sophist*, the Peripatetic historical picture that determines the doxography had a decisive prefiguration in which the stranger asks about originary being in such a way that he calculates and enumerates how many originary beings there are and what is to be accepted as such (*Sophist* 242c–243b). This is the very question frame entrusted to us from Aristotle that occurs in the first book of the *Physics*, in particular (albeit in a manner that is still too argumentative). It seems to me that the correspondence that exists here between Aristotle and the scheme of the *Sophist* makes it quite likely that the *Sophist* depicts, albeit with an ironic veneer, a well-known line of reasoning from Platonic teaching.[25]

The second observation, which becomes evident precisely through these depictions in *Sophist*, concerns our old problem of becoming and being, cosmogony and cosmology. What the Eleatic stranger, with ironic respect, had to reveal to the imaginative genealogists is that these joyfully inventive narrators of births and marriages were themselves too good to be concerned with the simplistic understanding of their contemporaries. They did not say what it actually means for being to come to be in this way. As I see it, this is an indirect testimony that all these stories of the becoming, begetting, and originating of being that in and of themselves serve the theogonical schematism certainly wanted nothing else but to make being comprehensible—and yet, precisely in this way, also to let it remain incomprehensible.

That is, there seems to be a complete disjunction presented by the concepts of stillness and motion, and the stranger asks—as if it were the very height of difficulty—how being itself is supposed to show itself outside of these two things (*Sophist* 250 d). Undoubtedly, it is this difficulty concerning being that Heidegger referred to in *Being and Time*. But here, obviously, 'being' does not mean that dimension of *alêthêia* whose concealedness, according to Heidegger, constitutes the essence of metaphysics— here, rather, 'being' means all of that which is—which must be either static or in motion—and it points toward everything of which we *say* that it is, thus toward being that is encountered in the *logos*, being that does not let itself be grasped in the opposition of stillness and motion.

Even here we could say that the reconstruction of the Eleatic concept of being into the guiding idea of the *logos* had still not been driven forward to an adequate conceptuality. The multiplicity that has entered into being and makes possible the pluralism of ideas is no doubt based principally upon the recognition

25. The irony of the turn of phrase, *hêmin ôligôrêsan*, (*Sophist* 243 a 6) returns literally in Aristotle's *Metaphysics* B 4, 1000 a 10 (which is employed against the Theologians). Is this a citation from the *Sophist*? Or perhaps from *Plato* himself?

of non-being in being; but in Plato this non-being vacillates between the formal category of being-other and the content category of change or, as the case may be, movement. This is exactly the point, however, at which Aristotle first pushes through toward the complete dissolution of the Eleatic limitations on being. He interprets non-being within the realm of the content determination of beings as 'possibility toward being' or, in other words, as the absence of that which constitutes complete being, that is, the 'not-yet' of the *eidos*.

Here is where the decisive step that takes Aristotle beyond the Pythagoreanism of the *Timaeus* shows itself. He recognizes that the ordering of nature is, in itself, not adequately determined if in it we conceive the illusion of an intelligible cosmos within what is limited yet indeterminate (the old Pythagorean oppositional pair of *peras* and *apeiron*). What Aristotle sees, rather, is that the opposition of not-yet-being and the complete presence of the *eidos* is not the abstract opposition of the indeterminate and its determination, but instead that the not-yet itself belongs within the sphere of the *eidos* and, as 'steresis,'[26] it presents a particular 'look' that beings provide for it, and he also sees that this co-constitutes the real being of nature. The *technê* model is characteristically reformulated by this, not to the extent that the finished product is the actual existing thing 'in itself' as ready to use (as is the case in *technê*), but rather it is that which is present in its coming forth.[27] It is nature in each of its phases. Nature is not really *technê*, even if one can define it as that which produces itself. For it is not like an artist, who can produce this or that thing as he wishes from out of the arbitrariness of his materials (albeit 'suitable' materials). This applies as well: the material is 'not yet' the work; but this 'not-yet' is a different one from the not-yet of natural things that ripen toward their maturity or fill the scope of their 'natural' motion. Plato's way of thinking the being of *technê* cannot completely redeem this. 'Actual' nature is not an obscuring of true being as it (nature) must take the illusion of intelligible structures in a contradictory medium into account—it is the being of the things themselves as they are from their origin on. So the meaning of the *archê*, the beginning, and the origin that dominates early thinking

26. ['negation' or 'privation']
27. [*das im Hervorkommen Befindliche*]

The Beginning of Knowledge

reproduces itself in Aristotle in that Aristotle differentiates him-self from the *technê* model of the Platonic fable. Nevertheless, he wrests his way of conceiving things from *technê* and thereby imposes the concept of *hylê* upon early thought, a concept that, to Aristotle, is totally inadequate.

5

Greek Philosophy and Modern Thought

Greek philosophy and modern thought—this is a topic that has posed itself to German philosophy in particular from the very beginning. People have even spoken of the 'Greco-mania' of the German philosophers, and this term is surely not just applicable to Heidegger or the Marburg school of neo-Kantianism. It is just as valid for the great movement of German Idealism, in which Fichte, Schelling, and Hegel—inspired by Kant—undertook an immediate turn back toward the thought-provoking ideas of Platonic and Aristotelian dialectic. Nevertheless, in a peculiar way, such a confrontation is an ambiguous challenge for modern thinking. On the one hand, we should never forget that Greek philosophy is not philosophy in that narrow sense that we associate with the word today. Philosophy meant the whole of theoretical and, therefore, scientific interest, and there is no doubt that it was the Greeks who instigated a world-historical decision with their own thinking and decided the path of modern civilization with the creation of science. What separates the occident, Europe, the so-called 'Western world,' from the great hieratic cultures of the Asian countries is precisely this new awakening of the desire to know with which Greek philosophy, Greek mathematics, Greek medicine, and the whole of their theoretical curiosity and their intellectual mastery is associated. Thus, for modern thinking, the confrontation with Greek thinking is a kind of self-encounter for us all.

In this thinking, humanity's 'being there at home' in the world[1] signifies the inner correspondence between 'coming to be at home'[2] and the 'making oneself at home'[3] that characterizes the craftsman, the expert, the creator of new shapes and forms, the *technites*, the man who masters a technique and at the same time finds his proper place. This is why it requires the discovery of a free space for creative production that will be available to him in the middle of a pre-given nature, a wholeness of the world that orders itself in shapes and forms. Thus, philosophy during the Greek awakening is the thoughtful becoming aware of the enormous exposure of human beings within the 'there,'[4] within this tiny field of free space that the ordered whole of the course of nature allows for human will and human ability. But it is precisely this exposure that thinking becomes conscious of and that leads it to pose such monstrous questions as: What was in the beginning? What does it mean to say that something is? What does it mean to say that nothing is? Is nothing something? The posing of these questions is the beginning of Greek philosophy, and the basic answers are: *physis* ('there-being-from-out-of-itself'[5] in the ordering of the whole) and *logos*, (the insight into and insightfulness of this whole, including even the *logos* of human craftsmanship). But, in this way, the image of Greek philosophy in confrontation with modern science is fixed there almost like an antipode and not just as a precursor to and a discloser of the course of theoretical ability and mastery. It is the confrontation between the intelligible world and the masterable world that we become aware of in Greek thinking.

This was the great collapse that began in the seventeenth century with the creation of Galilean mechanics, with the reflection of a new resolve for and new paths to knowledge by the great scientists and thinkers of the seventeenth century. The world was now the object of methodical inquiry by means of the mathematically conceived and abstracted and isolated question frame of modern experimental science. If we wanted to express this innovation formulaically, we could say that it was the abandonment

1. [*das Daheimsein des Menschen in der Welt*]
2. [*Heimischwerden*]
3. [*sich heimisch Machen*]
4. [*in das Da*]
5. [*Von-sich-aus-Da-Sein*]

of the anthropomorphism of the Greek contemplation of the world. As wonderfully simple and convincing as the physics of the Aristotelian tradition was—the physics, that is, that tells us that fire goes up because it is its nature to want to be up and the stone falls downward because it is only at home when it is down—this interpretation of nature, articulated from the perspective of human beings and their self-understanding, was, as we know and as no one who belongs to our modern world can conceal, an anthropomorphic covering for the possibilities of grasping and mastering the world through knowledge.

If modern science were constituted not by arbitrary subsequent interests, but rather by the proper form of its global access to technology (to forming, making, changing, constructing), then the heritage of ancient philosophy would nevertheless persist alongside it—in the obvious fact that we both want and need to see our world as understandable rather than just masterable. In opposition to the constructivism of the modern sciences, which only accepts as known and understood what it can reproduce, the Greek conception of science is characterized by *physis*, that is, by the horizon of the existence of the order of things that shows itself out of itself and regulates itself. Thus the question that is posed for us by the confrontation of modern thinking with this Greek heritage is to what extent this ancient heritage offers a truth that remains concealed from us under the peculiar epistemological conditions of modernity.

If we wanted to indicate the distinction that unfolds itself here with a single word, that word would be 'object.'[6] In the concept of cognition—at least in the English terms, 'object' and 'objectivity'[7]—there seems to be a self evident presupposition that we can know 'objects,'[8] that is, that we can bring them to knowledge in their proper being in the manner of an objective cognition.[9] The question assigned to us by the ancient tradition and the ancient heritage is the extent to which there are limitations posed by this enterprise of objectification.[10] Is there

---

6. [*Gegenstand*]
7. [Here Gadamer actually says, "*in dem Fremdwort* (the foreign words) *Objekt und Objektivität*"]
8. [*Gegenstände*]
9. [*einer objektiven Erkenntnis*]
10. [*Vergegenständlichung*]

a non-objectivity that, in principle, eludes the clutches of modern science with an inner material necessity? With a few demonstrations, I will try to illustrate that it is indeed the relevant and persistent heritage of Greek thinking to be conscious of the limits of objectification.

To me, the guiding example for this topic seems to be the experience of the body. What we call 'body' is most certainly not the *res extensa* of the Cartesian definition of *corpus*. The body does not manifest itself by sheer mathematical extendedness. It is perhaps inaccessible to objectification in an essential way. For how do human beings encounter corporeality? Do they not encounter it as standing over against them (and therefore in its possible objectivity) only when its function is disrupted? Corporeality announces itself as the disturbance of being given over to one's own being alive in sickness, discomfort, and so on. The conflict that is set up between natural bodily experience (that mysterious process in which well being and health go unnoticed) and the strain of keeping illness at bay through the process of objectification is experienced by everyone who is placed in the situation of the object, the situation of a patient being treated by technical means. It is an expression of the self-understanding of our modern medical science to render these disturbances, these insurrections against our corporeality that offer themselves up for objectification, masterable with the tools of modern science.

In fact, the concepts of 'objectivity' and 'object'[11] are so alien to the immediate understanding in which human beings seek to make themselves at home in the world that, characteristically, the Greeks did not even have terms for them. They could barely even speak of a 'thing.' The Greek word that they were in the habit of using in this whole area is the word *pragma*, which, as foreign words go, is not entirely foreign to us and which refers to that within which we are entangled in the praxis of living; thus it refers not to that which stands over against us or opposed to us as something to be overcome, but rather to that within which we move and that with which we have to do. This is an orientation that has been marginalized by the modern global mastery that is structured by science and the technology that grounds it.

11. [*'Gegenständlichkeit' und 'Gegenstand'*]

A second example—and I am choosing an especially provocative one—is the *freedom* of human beings. It, too, has the structure of what I have described as 'essential non-objectivity.'[12]
Admittedly, this has never been completely forgotten; and, with
complete consciousness of the basic orientation of modern science
and it epistemological possibilities—and in direct opposition
to them—the greatest thinker of the idea of freedom who ever
lived (Kant, I mean) developed the idea that freedom is not grasp-
able and provable by these epistemological possibilities. Freedom
is not a fact in nature but rather (as he formulated it in a chal-
lenging paradox) a fact of reason,[13] something we must think,
because without thinking of ourselves as free we cannot understand ourselves at all. Freedom is the fact of reason.[14]

In the realm of human action, however, this is not the only
limiting case for all objectivity. I think the Greeks had it right
when they placed the idea of being shaped by society,[15] *ethos*,
alongside the fact of reason. *Ethos* is the term that Aristotle
coined for this. The possibility of conscious choice and free
decision is always accompanied by something that we always
already are—and we are not an 'object' to ourselves. It seems to
me to be one of the great legacies of Greek thought for our own
thinking that, on this basis of actual lived life, Greek ethics
allowed ample space for a phenomenon that, in modernity, is
hardly ever given as theme of philosophical reflection—I mean the
theme of friendship, 'philia.' This is a word that has such narrow
conceptual resonance for us that we first must broaden it in
order to know what was generally meant by it. Perhaps it will
suffice to recall the famous Pythagorean saying, 'Among friends,
everything is shared.' In philosophical reflection, friendship is a
term for solidarity. Solidarity, however, is a form of world experience and social reality that one cannot plan for by forced
objectification or produce through artificial institutions. For,
on the contrary, solidarity precedes all possible concerns and
effects of institutions, economic systems, judicial systems, and
social mores, sustains them, and makes them possible. If anyone

12. [*essentielle Ungegenständlichkeit*]
13. [*ein Vernunftfaktum*]
14. [*das Faktum der Vernunft*]
15. [*das gesellschaftliche Geformtsein*]

knows this, it is the jurist. On the other hand, this seems to me to be an aspect of the truth that Greek thinking, in this case, keeps in reserve for modern thinking.

And now a third phenomenon related to this one: I mean the role that *self-consciousness* plays in modern thinking. As we all know, it is pivotal for modern thought that self-consciousness has methodological primacy. For us, methodological knowledge is a self-conscious procedure that accomplishes each step with self-control. Thus, ever since Descartes, self-consciousness has been the point at which philosophy secures its ultimate evidentness and, at the same time, the certainty of science secures its most extreme legitimation. But were the Greeks not justified when they saw that self-consciousness was secondary with respect to that phenomenon of having submitted to and being open to the world[16]—the phenomenon that we call consciousness, knowledge, openness to experience? Was it not precisely the development of modern science that taught us to harbor doubts about the assertions of self-consciousness? In regard to the radical doubt that is the fundament of Cartesian knowledge, Nietzsche said: it must be doubted even more fundamentally. Freud taught us how many of our basic inclinations screen themselves off from us within our self-consciousness. Critiques of society and ideology have shown us how many of the certainties that self-consciousness held to be self evident and unquestionable are reflections of completely different interests and realities. In short: the fact that self-consciousness possesses the unquestionable primacy assigned to it by modern thinking can justly be doubted. Here, too, it appears to me that, in that magnificent self-forgetfulness with which it thinks of its own faculty for thinking, its own experience of the world, as the wide open eye of the intellect, Greek thinking holds in reserve a principal contribution toward limiting the illusions of self-knowledge.

Continuing on from this point, let us take one last thing into consideration, something that has come entirely to the fore in the discussions of contemporary philosophy and that, in any case, can be held fast by the concepts of objectivity and objectification only by means of force and violence: I am talking about the phenomenon of *language*. Language, it seems to me, is one of

16. [*der Welthingegebenheit und Weltoffenheit*]

the most compelling phenomena of non-objectivity insofar as essential self-forgetfulness characterizes the performative character of speech. It is always already a technical distortion when the modern thematizing of language sees in it an *instrumentarium*, a system of signs, an arsenal of tools for communication, as if we kept these instruments or tools of speech—words and sentence structure—handy in some kind of storage and simply had to apply them to whatever we encountered. Here, the Greek counter-example is overwhelmingly evident. The Greeks had no word for language at all. They only had a word for the tongue (*glotta*— that which calls forth sounds) and a word for that which is communicated by language: *logos*. With the *logos*, precisely that upon which the inner self-forgetfulness of speech is essentially drawn is pushed into view—the world itself, which is evoked by speech, lifted into presence, and brought into articulation and communicative participation. In speaking about things, the things are there; it is in speech and speaking with one another that the world and the experiential world of human beings constructs itself and not in an objectification that (vis-à-vis the communicative transmission of the insights of one person to the insights of another) bases itself on objectivity and purports to be knowledge for everyone. The articulation of the experiential world in *logos*, discourse with one another, the communicative sedimentation of our experiential world that encompasses everything that we can exchange with one another, forms a kind of knowledge that, alongside the great monologue of the modern sciences and their growing accumulation of empirical potential, still presents the other half of the truth. The theme of the confrontation between the modern idea of science and the Greek conceptions of philosophy thus possesses an enduring relevance. For it deals with the integration of the magnificent results and the faculties/achievements of the modern empirical sciences into social consciousness, into the life experience of the individual and the group. In the end, however, this integration does not come about through the methods of modern science and its mode of unwavering self-control. It accomplishes itself in the praxis of social life itself. It must always take back into its own purview that which has been placed in the power of human beings, and it has to vindicate the limits that human reason has placed upon its own power and recklessness. We require no proof to see that, for the contemporary human being as well (even as much as modern industry and technology are spreading across the entire globe), in this sense, the understandable world, the world in which we are at home, remains the final authority.

6

Natural Science and the Concept of Nature

This topic is of particular concern to a scholar who has chosen the ancient world as one of his most important fields of study, but it also concerns our present age—the age of science and the dominance of the industrial revolution. At the same time it becomes the starting point for a fundamentally skeptical question: whether or not Greek science is science in the same sense as the modern natural sciences are. Indeed, we have learned to view the path of research in the modern sciences as a historical topic, and, moreover, ever since Thomas Kuhn, we speak of revolutions in the sciences rather than sheer progress. The famous aforementioned book, *The Structure of Scientific Revolutions*, is nevertheless introduced by its author with the surprising motivation that, for him, Aristotelian physics presents such an obvious whole that the modern sciences (in contrast to the Aristotelian) in all of the diversity of their revolutions present but a single large revolution. I venture to add the question: Are they both sciences in the same sense? What does science mean now, and what did it mean then? Are they really two faces of the same science, and could there really be a confrontation between them?

The question pushes itself to the fore with a double obtrusiveness since we can no longer delimit our question by the European horizon within which Europe has acknowledged and nurtured its own Greek heritage. Today, modern science is a global reality. It certainly began in Europe, but today its influence on the ways of life in cultural regions other than the European cannot be neglected. In the modern world, since cultures much older than the European one have begun to live with the results and consequences of modern science, the Greek heritage that was succeeded by Europe and its scientific culture finds itself faced with entirely new confrontations. Our question, therefore, will not depend entirely upon that single confrontation that can be traced back to European history and its modern development. On the contrary, we certainly cannot overlook the fact that standing in the background of this question is the confrontation between our own world (with its Christian origins) and non-European cultural regions (with their different religious traditions) that we have begun to live alongside of. This is, of course, an even broader topic, one that also puts the ecumenical mission of the Christian Gospel to the test. It is all the more important, therefore, to question ourselves about the emergence of modern science and its Greek origins. Europe, as such, did not even exist back then. In the beginning, Greece, that little country whose cultural heritage we carry with us, was itself only a marginal figure alongside such great cultures as the Egyptians, the Persians, and the Babylonians. Only in our century did the early pre-Greek era (in its full scope and in the abundance of its of culture and tradition) come within the purview of European scholarship. We have gained an essential insight from it concerning the beginning of philosophy in Greece. Meanwhile, we know much about Egyptian mathematics and astronomy and no less about Babylonian mathematics and what their astronomy was about; thus, traces of the earliest astronomical observations from indefinite periods are really scattered across the entire planet. From this last perspective we are even directed back far beyond any and all linguistic tradition.

Now, is this supposed to mean that science is that much older, or must we ask ourselves whether science does not have a special meaning for us that, in the end, allowed it to become the destiny of European—or perhaps even the destiny of humanity? Moreover, it is not just science whose beginnings are at issue here. It is, at the same time, the concept of philosophy, which is intimately connected with Greek science. We would be hard pressed to name more important circumstantial evidence for the novelty of this question of a European beginning than the significance of the alphabet, whose origins and development are connected with the Greek beginnings in the most intimate way.

We are still at the beginning of our ruminations about this area of study. It is not just a question of the written tradition, which has broadened our horizon since the deciphering of cuneiform writing. It is, above all, a question of the rapid reception and development of the alphabet, which opens up the literary tradition of Greek culture. Thus, we see ourselves immediately directed back toward how the Greeks themselves thought about beginnings; and if there is any one thing that best illuminates their own situation, then it has to be the famous answer that Solon was supposed to have been given in Egypt as he tried to inform himself about the beginnings, heritage, and past of that culture. According to Plato, he received the famous answer: "You Greeks are still children" and therefore naive about, ignorant of, and ill-suited to the centuries and millennia fading away into the darkness of the past.

Let us consult the master of those who know such things, and that is Aristotle. He ascribes the beginning of philosophy to the culture of Miletus. According to Aristotle, after all, it is totally uncertain whether or nor the first one who is supposed to have pursued philosophy in Miletus left any written record of his thinking at all. Nevertheless, we do know approximately when the culture of Miletus had its rise and how this rise is connected with the colonial era during which the entire Mediterranean culture and its coastline were populated with Greek settlements and new establishments. But if we now seek Aristotle's advice, then we must deal at once with a long and very extensive chain of tradition. Above all, it is Aristotelian physics itself and the commentaries on it that, to a large degree, form the basis of our knowledge about the origins of philosophy. Indeed, there can be no doubt that the written record of the epic tradition (i.e., Homer and Hesiod) already falls within the age of literacy. There is no question that the aftereffects of Homeric language and the aftereffects of Hesiod's cosmogonical tales co-determined the bourgeoning civic culture of the Greek colonial period. Ever since then, Aristotle and the scholastic and history-shaping force associated with his thinking have not only remained the source of our knowledge, but they also indicate the tutelary heritage of our understanding.

Aristotle certainly distinguished the first 'theologians' explicitly from the first of the philosophers, who was, according to him, Thales of Miletus. However, Aristotle himself had provided the concepts with which he would conceive the beginnings of science and philosophy. Thus, nearly everyone is given to understand that, for Thales, in the beginning there was water, out of which the other elements—earth and air and the shining warmth of the stars—developed. Aristotle coined the term 'matter,' *hylê*, for all of these. This, of course, is anything but an appropriate schema for the first philosophy of the West. Because of the distinction that Aristotle had bestowed upon him, it was unavoidable that in subsequent eras Thales would be shrouded in legend, and thus we will never know how much of it antedates this distinction. However much we want to find the path from its first beginning in water to the whole of the universe, we find hardly a hint of this in the Thales of the Aristotelian reports. At best, there is one observation pointing back to the water thesis that sounds originary—the idea that water carries the earth. There could be a genuine observation in this in which water refers to the primal that carries the solid land. After all, it does carry everything that is not too heavy to float on the water. The plank floating on the water seems to me like a first hint of the puzzle of an equilibrium that always seeks to reproduce itself. No matter how deeply we push the plank under, it will always rise to surface again. I only pursue this in order to find any possible connection at all with the priority of water in Aristotle's text without bringing into play the later concept of matter and with it the doctrine of causes, which is very far removed from this.

Besides, it is well understood that, as one of the great sages of Greece, Thales has traditionally been attributed with the widest variety of qualities and merits. Yet, an anecdote that was meant polemically might be the most suitable one in that early world of beginnings. It is the story in which Thales is supposed to have fallen into a well, which was apparently dry, and was helped out of it by a Thracian woman. The story only has a point, however, if we assume that Thales climbed into the dry well in order to observe the stars from there. This was, undoubtedly, a more precise means of stargazing than was otherwise possible. The well was something like the telescope of the time. In any case, we know that the world of the stars had been observed from time immemorial in all of the most disparate regions of the earth.

There is, however, yet another point that compels us to take the old reports about Thales serious, and that is the information concerning his knowledge of mathematics. It is clear, at any rate, that he learned from others in this field—land surveying from the Egyptians and the long record of solar and lunar eclipses from the Babylonians. So here we can chalk up at least one certain result—namely, that (in contrast to the mathematics of Egypt and of Asia minor) the concept of proof, the concept of science, received its decisive characterization for the first time with Thales. Science is only true knowledge when it can be proven. To what extent such logical demands could be carried out at that time in the field of mathematics is beside the point here. But it seems certain that neither the superior knowledge of the Egyptians nor that of the Babylonians was at all interested in anything like the provability of mathematical principles. To them, everything was solely a matter of practical application. It seems that here, in Miletus, a first distinguishing characteristic of science shows itself. Science consists not merely in knowledge but also in precisely the kind of logical necessities that we know from proofs in the field of mathematics.

Our knowledge of Anaximander, the other great thinker from Miletus, is very much richer. From him we even have a written statement that has been handed down, one that has been the object of innumerable interpretations ever since Theophrastus. It is the famous passage about coming into being and passing away: that all of the things that are must account for and pay penance to one another according to the injunction of time. At one time, this proposition was most popular among writers like Schopenhauer and Nietzsche. For the 'one another' was missing from the transmitted text, and so one could understand the statement as though an individual, having isolated itself, had to pay penance for its isolation by its downfall and its return to the infinite. Since the original text with its 'one another' has been restored, however, what resonates for us in the proposition is not so much the romantic crisis of the Enlightenment and the approaching nihilism as it is the true essence of nature. Everything reestablishes itself in the ordered return of day and night or summer and winter. Because we have an equilibrium here that always reestablishes itself within itself, this is a first inkling of what we, too, would perhaps like to call 'nature.'

It would be going too far at this point to debate the entire existing doxography on Anaximander. The only thing we can really say for certain is that Anaximander could have put forward neither a cosmogony nor a cosmology without the example of Hesiod's *Theogony* and (as Uvo Hölscher has shown) in accordance with the Asian model. We must, of course, keep at arm's length the common misconception that the *apeiron* (the limitless or the infinite) would have been intended as a superior, abstractly formed sensible substance between the water of Thales and the air of Anaximenes. This does nothing but demonstrate how inappropriate the Aristotelian concept of *hylê* is for Milesian school! Nevertheless, the fact that a cosmology was developed here in all its particulars leads us to the point at which the philosophical problems of world creation and world order became a challenge for thinking.

This is the new stage in which the Eleatic philosophers and their critics took such conceptual modes as coming into being and passing away as their standard. We are finally on solid ground here thanks to the diligence of Simplicius; one of the great scholars of Byzantine Athens, he copied and commented on large parts of Parmenides' didactic poem before the Academy was dissolved. This, at least in its rough form, is the only thinking prior to all Aristotelian and modern thought that has been recognizably transmitted to us. Even this, of course, is really just a matter of one small fragment. Nevertheless, this one fragment is the almost completely intact introduction to the great doctrine of Parmenides. Of course, what follows from there is primarily the development of a physics for mortals, a physics which the goddess commends to the mortals. Only a few fragments of this later part are intact. Nevertheless, we have to free ourselves from the impression that only the intact first part matters and that we could really reconstruct the whole of Parmenides' thought from it. We might call this introduction to the didactic poem 'logic' or 'ontology' and perhaps conceive of what follows from it as a kind of cosmology. But what matters here is precisely what the goddess puts into the mouths of the mortals, whereby she distinguishes herself from the other great thinkers who had developed their new worldview at the time in Miletus. Only at this point does it really become clear what the great vision was that was placed in Parmenides' mouth by 'the goddess.' That is, the discourse here is not just about a divine wisdom that repudiates all non-being as nonsense, and thus it is not just about the critique of coming into being and passing away and of the indestructible presence of the well-rounded sphere of being. Rather, the discourse (with a slight tone of condescension and not without some critical irony) is of the only possible way to conceive of the many, that is, from the opposition of day and night, of light and dark, which constitutes the multiplicity of appearances. And without the idea that we must therefore conceive of either a self-changing being or a non-being! Things appear to be different in the sheer difference between daylight and nightly darkness. The isolated statement from Parmenides that Aristotle cited and that was handed down as Fragment 16 fits very well here: "Just as the mixture of the limbs comports itself in each case, so awareness presents itself to human beings. For it is always the same thing that perceives in each and every human being, the nature of the limbs—what we are aware of is the 'more'."

I do not want to draw any precipitous consequences or infer any corrections that might ensue from a precise reading of the transition in the only intact introduction to Parmenides' physics of mortals that we have. But, in any case, we have to place the accents differently than Plato and Aristotle did—certainly in such a way that the doctrine of the Platonic reference to Eleatic thinking does not directly contradict the introduction of the didactic poem—no more than the Aristotelian derivation of the later corpuscle theory does. Besides, Plato carries the doctrine of unity into the development of his dialectic *ad absurdum*, as the *Parmenides* dialogue shows, and Aristotle sees a valid aspect of the 'mixture' in that Parmenides, Anaxagoras, and Democritus all point in the same direction: differentiation is self-separation.[1]

Now, undoubtedly, there is also the ever-growing mathematical science to take into consideration, a science whose beginnings we found in Thales and which was certainly worked into the cosmogony and cosmology of Anaximander. The question of how the Pythagorean tradition deals with this incipient science of nature is more difficult. This is such a complex topic that we have to be satisfied with the idea that one unequivocal hint can be gleaned from Plato's comments. The Pythagorean doctrine of numbers proceeds from the fact that the harmony in the whole-number relationships that depend on the lengths of strings provides evidence for the ontological status of numbers[2] in the

1. [*Unterscheiden ist Sich-Scheiden*]
2. [*Seinsrang der Zahlen*]

Pythagorean doctrine. No doubt, this is precisely where Plato takes a new step when, by means of his concept of ideas, he overcomes the simple identification of number and being and dares to take a step beyond the ideality of mathematical truths, a step toward the ideality of the *logos* and the dialectic—without therefore becoming a Sophist. Number always remains that whereby Plato distinguishes the being of the idea from all appearing multiplicities. Even as it is carried out, however, the Platonic doctrine of ideas sees, as it were, no necessity to discuss how the things of nature in their individuality and their multiplicity actually participate in the being of ideas. The participation of the individual in the idea is not even the true participation from which the Platonic dialectic of the one and the many gains its scope. This true participation, rather, is the relationship of the ideas to one another and what Plato has in mind with the *logos*. The differentiation of mathematical being from the being of ideas is therefore incompatible with such a Pythagorean identity, and surely it was precisely the genius of Theaetetus that came to Plato's aid insofar as it offered him the tremendous advances of contemporary mathematics and even stereometry. Both are 'pure' mathematics for which Plato takes responsibility.

So we should not wonder that pure mathematical knowledge in all its clarity is invoked in the profoundly mythical playfulness of the *Timaeus*, a knowledge with the help of which Plato even ennobles the theory of atoms. His is, at any rate, the most radical form of the corpuscular theory. Democritus put this theory forward, but his name is never mentioned by Plato. Indeed, in the *Timaeus* everything has a mathematical form and everything is built upon the ideality of the mathematical being of the so-called Platonic bodies. Nevertheless, without trepidation, it is now treated once again as a theory of nature. Triangles are bundled together on top of one other and thereby achieve a natural corporeality all by themselves. This, of course, is part of the ingenious game in which scientific precision and childish naivete play into one another throughout the text.

Thus, in spite of what has happened in modern times due to the scientific success of the concept of the atom as atomic theory has prevailed in the physics of modern science (to the credit of Democritus), we should not forget the key position of the *Timaeus*. The Democritan theory of atoms was anything but mathematical, as the concept of the void already shows.

Therefore, it is no wonder that the truly productive minds of modern quantum physics have showed a sincere predilection for the *Timaeus*. The modern natural science that calls itself physics is really something completely different from the concept of *physis* that we find in the doctrines of the Aristotelian school. In fact, there one can hardly speak of an application of mathematics in the way that modern science has developed such applications as its foundation. Kant expressed it clearly: nature is nothing but 'matter subject to laws,' and this accurately describes the consummate form of Newtonian physics.

In truth, it was not really Plato's *Timaeus* but rather Aristotelian physics that dominated the whole of later antiquity right up to the dawn of modernity, and because Aristotelian physics encompasses the movement of everything natural it was actually a concept of nature that pushed itself forward here. It accords with the pattern of human life experience that even the cycle of nature is thought according to human behavior, which moves by itself and here and there as it will—fire moves itself up toward the stars, the falling rock down toward the other rocks. In Hellenistic times, the era dominated by Aristotle brought scientific advances in many areas. A complicated astronomy had become necessary in order to incorporate the irregular stars, the planets, into the cyclical star system of antiquity by a synthesis of their circular movements. Accordingly, one did not consider comets to be stars at all but rather meteors. This makes it clear that there was something so illuminating about the uniformity of daily life experience and the science of nature that neither in astronomy nor anywhere else—even in the Renaissance (that is with the revival of the Greek cultural world)—could this nascent study of nature separate itself from the uniformity of the Aristotelian picture of the world.

It is generally believed, of course, that modernity and its science took their decisive step with the Copernican revolution. The Canon of Thorn was certainly a good humanist and a shrewd thinker, and so he adopted the revolutionary idea that the sun does not move around the earth, but rather the earth goes around the sun. It occurred to Copernicus to document such sensory illusions quite beautifully with citations from Virgil. For him, however, the description of the movements of the stars themselves still remained completely within the framework of ancient astronomical theory. As the Church turned against the revolutionary idea of Copernicus in consideration of the Creation story, it was not totally without justification that Osiander explained and defended the heliocentric model as a harmless mathematical inversion. The road to a really new astronomical world view was first paved by Kepler, and it did not receive its true beginning with the spectacularly gigantic proportions of the stellar world at all. The real revolution, rather, began with the mechanics provided by Galileo. Even for the Church it could remain a completely harmless distinction—initially, that is, until Galileo publicly adopted the Copernican worldview in his dialogue about the two cosmological systems.

The true audacity of Galileo rested in his assertion that everything that falls does so according to the same laws and would fall at the same rate if not for the resistance of air. The awe-inspiring intellectual power of Galileo made it possible for him to perceive the free fall 'in his mind' (*mente percipio*) in such a way that the falling was in no way dependent upon the condition of the falling object. In a vacuum, a bar of lead falls no faster than a feather. In those days, no one could yet prove this through experimentation! The new audacity of the mathematically structured thinking that we call modern science was really this kind of departure from appearances. The real functional significance of mathematics was changed by this. It now served for the description of measurable values from which the structural cooperation of the measurable data of time and space and acceleration could be derived. These are the laws of free fall, and they are totally independent of the weight of the falling body. Mathematical abstraction thereby turned out to be the procedure that would prove itself over and over again in the mastering of the forces of nature. It first achieved perfection with Newton, who overcame the ancient patrimony—namely, the complete separation of the heavenly realm from the sublunar world. Only since Newton has there been one and the same science for the heavens and the earth.

In antiquity, mathematics was considered to be the real science, and, to that extent, 'science' was not really natural science, and it was not at all dependent upon experience. In the Hellenistic age, the Aristotelian school had an enormous effect in many technical fields of knowledge. Philosophy itself lost its comprehensive value and, like an immortal Socrates, concentrated itself more and more in the direction of practical philosophy. We need only think the effect of Epicurus on the Stoa. Greek philosophy was first placed in the service of Christian theology with late Neoplatonism and its affect on the Church Fathers (inspired, in part, by the Arabic transmission of Aristotelian physics). This is what we call Scholasticism, and it is what laid the ground, in the age of the Renaissance, humanism, and the Reformation, for the emergence of the new sciences—jurisprudence and medicine, in particular. In those days, the progress of the modern natural sciences occurred less in the universities. The real scientists were not to be found at these scholastically dominated schools—not even Leibniz, who, after all, set about the highly consequential task of bringing Greek philosophy and modern science together.

In this epoch of enlightenment, as the science of modernity began its triumphal procession, we can understand how the limitations of the new science also soon became detectible under these circumstances. Already in Descartes' century, Pascal spoke of two kinds of spirit: the 'esprit géométrique' and the 'esprit de finesse.' 'Geometry' had clear priority in the scientific consciousness of the time. Even the 'geometrical' gardens of the eighteenth century were replaced only recently by the more natural 'English gardens.' Thus, under the technical progress of the sciences, natural philosophy was more and more driven out of the philosophical consciousness. This driving out process has been effective to this day. This becomes quite obvious in the nomenclature for science in the various languages. The German word, 'Wissenschaft,' was itself not yet the univocal term for the new science until two hundred years ago. One could speak of something that one knew, for instance, because one had already experienced it once: "Yes, I have knowledge [*Wissenschaft*] of that." On the other hand, in the Anglo-Saxon world the term 'science' is generally only applicable to the natural sciences. What Germans call the '*Geisteswissenschaften*' is called the 'humanities' here or, in France, 'lettres.' These are, in fact, laborious substitutions that—unlike the German concept of the *Geisteswissenschaften*—acknowledge the monopolistic place of the natural sciences.

This was exactly how the concept of method (as it appears in the title of Descartes' famous work, *Discours de la Methode*) first made science science. This new conception of science then found its culmination in Newton under the title, *Philosophiae naturalis principia mathematica*. In truth, this was not 'philosophy' in our sense, but rather a physics extended to the entire solar system. It then found its philosophical justification in Kant's *Critique of Pure Reason*, which 'crushed' all 'dogmatic metaphysics' with its critique. For Kant himself, however, this was not the decisive part of his philosophy. This consisted, rather, in the reestablishment of metaphysics, but on a new ground—the postulate of freedom. Nevertheless, the reappropriation of Kantianism in the nineteenth century had only the *Critique of Pure Reason* in mind. This created such a privileged position for the work that Kant's moral philosophy hardly attracted any attention outside of Germany, and even today it is confronted by baseless prejudices.

The same is true for German Idealism as a whole. In the trinity of Fichte, Schelling, and Hegel (in the wake of Leibniz and Kant) the task of comprehending the whole of the sciences became an all-encompassing system of philosophy under the title that Hegel had chosen: "Encyclopedia of the Philosophical Sciences." Schelling had already recently incorporated natural philosophy into his philosophy as the physical proof of transcendental idealism, and Hegel followed suit. Nevertheless, under the nineteenth-century ascendency of natural scientific research, natural philosophy was quickly forgotten (perhaps even too quickly). In any case, the age of the science of nature or of history was no age for philosophy. It is telling enough that in the post-Hegelian epoch the well-known distinction between the natural sciences and the human sciences has become a constant theme and has tried to ground the sciences philosophically as 'epistemology.'

With this, I have reached a point at which the question of a confrontation between the science of antiquity with the science of modernity—in the very posing of the question—has already become doubtful. These are precisely two very different conceptions of science, and I do not think we can verify it as a conceptual distinction by means of the concept of nature itself. This lies directly at the heart of the concept of scientific method, which itself even makes the application of a difference between the natural sciences and the human sciences questionable.

This is the extent of my exposition of the ancient background of the European concept of science, the concept through which European culture dominates the entire globe. People are constantly trying to bring the unity of science to bear against its differences, and this holds true even for the problematic to which our present discussion is dedicated. If we look only to the position of modern physics, then we cannot help but recognize the ancient heritage within it, a heritage that is present, above all, in the development of mathematics. On the other hand, the concept of nature itself has rarely been a theme of the sciences as such. Rather, we count it as an episode in middle-European intellectual history that Rousseau's critique of the Enlightenment and its intellectual arrogance was heard all across Europe. German Romanticism became the heartland from out of which even the human sciences received their particular stamp. In Hölderlin, we find the line, "Nature has now awakened with the force of arms." One could hardly have heard anything like this again in the middle of our century. In reaction to the industrial revolution, a new flourishing of technocracy and its accompanying bureaucracy first led to a reappropriation of the concept of nature, which we all know by the ecological catchphrase, 'the conservation of nature.' In our century, the leading natural scientific disciplines (without which the situation of the sciences is quite unthinkable) continue to be physics, the theory of relativity, and quantum physics. Here, the problems at the limits of the measuring sciences have eliminated the last vestige of intuitiveness by means of the complete mathematical formulation of physics. The concept of nature in philosophy has been replaced by symmetrical equations.

It will be our task to discuss whether or not the situation of today's natural sciences can also (among its other new emphases) lead to a new kind of confrontation with the ancient heritage of science. Today, to a certain extent, one could expect biochemistry (which currently deals with problems that we associate with the concept of *physis*—living, growing nature) to be placed at the center of research interests. But it could be that the discredited philosophy of nature, in addition to remembering the ancient concept of *physis*, will make new problem horizons visible. This remains to be seen. One thing we should not expect from this, however, is that the opposition between the natural sciences and the human sciences could be diminished by incorporating the dimension of time and the evolution of the universe. The opposite is the case. Since with our new interests we know more and more about the history of the universe and about process and reality,[3] we become clearly conscious once again of the complete otherness of that world of knowledge constructed upon memory, remembrance, and tradition—the 'life world'—and, along with it, even the so-called human sciences. Both the religious and the philosophical heritage of our Western culture come to life in this world again and again.

In a certain sense, however, we should not see the otherness of the human sciences as being directly opposed to the natural sciences. And the human sciences are not about romantic dreams either. We should not forget: it is nature itself that has impelled us towards culture. Thus, the fact that we cannot survive without culture continues to be true as well.

3. [Here Gadamer uses the English words "process" and "reality."]

Publication History

"On the Tradition of Heraclitus" was first published as "Zur Überlieferung Heraklits" in *Sein und Geschichtlichkeit. Festschrift für Karl-Heinz Volkmann Schluck*, Frankfurt am Main, 1974, pp. 3–14. It was reprinted in GW 6: *Griechische Philosophie II*, pp. 232–241 under the title "Vom Anfang bei Heraklit." It was then reprinted in *Der Anfang des Wissens* as "Zur Überlieferung Heraklits."

"Heraclitus Studies" was originally presented as a lecture for a class in the philosophy of history at the Heidelberger Akademie der Wissenschaften on February 11, 1984. It was then published in GW 7: *Griechische Philosophie III: Plato im Dialog*, pp. 43–82, under the title "Heraklit Studien."

"Ancient Atomic Theory" was first published as "Antike Atomtheorie" in the *Zeitschrift für die gesamte Naturwissenschaft* 1 (1935–36), pp. 81–95. It was then reprinted in GW 5: *Griechische Philosophie I*, pp. 263–279.

"Plato and Presocratic Cosmology" was first published as "Platon und die vorsokratische Kosmologie" in *Epimeleia. Festschrift für Helmut Kuhn*, Munich, 1964, pp. 127–142. It was reprinted in GW 6, pp. 58–70, under the title "Platon und die Vorsokratiker."

"Greek Philosophy and Modern Thought" was first published as "Die griechische Philosophie und das moderne Denken" in *Festschrift für Franz Wieacker zum 70. Geburtstag*, edited by O. Berends, et al., Göttingen, 1978, pp. 361–365. It was then reprinted in GW 6, pp. 3–8.

"Natural Science and the Concept of Nature" was originally published as "Der Naturbegriff bei den Griechen in der modernen Physik" in *Colloquium Philosophicum. Annali del Dipartimento di Filosofia* 1 (1994/95), pp. 9–22. It was republished in *Der Anfang des Wissens* under the title "Der Naturbegriff und die Naturwissenschaft."

Index